Sedona Vortex Medium

By

Sonny Cemalovic

Amazon Kindle Publishing Inc.

© 2020 Sonny Cemalovic

Published in 2020

ISBN 9781676297116
Imprint: Independently published

~ To all souls that call Sedona home~

Table of Contents

Sedona Vortex Revealed   7

The story of Sedona   16

Pueblos in History   18

Sinagua   23

Sinagua the Ancient Americans   38

Sinagua and Hohokam   42

Sinagua and Patayan   47

Sinagua and Mogollon   51

Sinagua and Anasazi   57

The Tuzigoot Phase   63

Montezuma Castle   73

Montezuma Well   79

V-Bar-V   82

Sacred Mountain   86

Red Tank Draw   88

Honanki   91

Palatki   100

Shaman's Cave   109

Fay Canyon   112

Boynton Canyon Vortex   115

Arizona Creation   118

Red Rock Crossing   121

Cathedral Rock   124

Bell Rock Vortex   127

Baby Bell   129

Chapel of the Holy Cross   130

Cow Pies   134

Airport Vortex   137

Wind Tunnels   140

Soldier's Pass, Devil's Kitchen, Seven Sacred Pools, Brins Mesa 143

Indian Gardens and Oak Creek Canyon   145

West Fork Trail Vortex   147

Broken Arrow, Devil's Dining Room, Submarine Rock   150

Bradshaw Ranch   152

Seven Canyons   154

Application   156

Preparation   165

Dream   169

Remembering the Dream   175

Interpretation of dreams   177

Sanctuary   184

Christian Meditation   190

Method   197

Color Meditation   200

Balancing the Chakras   207

Balancing Chakras with Crystals   214

Out of body   221

Jewish Meditation   233

Intuition   240

Pendulum   247

Premonition   254

Precognition   257

Telepathy   267

Scrying   269

Mediumship   273

The Sedona Field   279

Third Eye   292

Vortex for you   295

Bibliography   298

*****

Sedona Vortex Revealed

There will be the first time in life for everything we experience and Sedona Vortex experience is the one that changed my life and will change yours once you visit her. What draws seven million people every year to this small town of fifteen thousand nestled high in the Northern Arizona Wilderness? Why all Native American tribes of the American Southwest come to the town of Sedona annually and where is that sacred ground they pay pilgrimage to? How the small hamlet of the two thousand that was unknown to the World in early 1970's became the most favourite international mecca for the New Age seekers, hikers, rock climbers, golfers, lovers, big Hollywood film fans, history buffs, UFO hunters, and numerous other visitors looking for the unknown? Where is exactly unknown and invisible treasure location that has been known to the Natives as the Great Red City Palatkwapi, which has been coined, the Vortex in 1986, by psychic Paige Bryant? Is Sedona is that promised land holding the secret of connecting the space and time in one unified invisible field that makes everybody's visit a life-changing event and brings first-time visitors back again? Sedona can be experienced with all your five senses and her vortex will help you experience the sixth one. Everybody has a six sense, deep down in our souls or in our subconsciousness that is locked and Sedona with its geo-magnetic fields help unlock the mystery that can't be explained neither with religion nor with science, yet. Sedona reveals and unlocks person's inner portal for bridging time-space and could change everything in that person's life, to the point that nothing was, is, or will be the same again. Sedona is a life-changing event, larger than a birth or death, marriage and divorce, health and sickness, pain and joy and any other major life experience. If religion is about organized faith, science is about an organized experiment. Sedona is beyond belief, scientific testing, it is about knowledge of self. This knowledge is not learnt, because it is already there, but it could be revealed and unlocked, pulled and retrieved from the dept of subconscious self.

When I visited Sedona for the first time, I knew anything about the town, less heard about the Vortex or its rich history of the Western movies story in Sedona, the Indian creation myths or archeological ruins, and I was not prepared to experience anything extraordinary or to take anything. I just wanted to have some good, fun time and experience what seven million people annually see in Sedona when they visited first-time alone or with the guided road tours from Las Vegas together with the Grand Canyon or even follow millions of Phoenicians in their short weekend getaway. I came from I-17 and took the 198 exit and after a few miles drive, saw the stunning rock formations that I have never seen before and would never see again. After the welcome center and green sleeping golf community of the Oak Creek Village that is small suburb of Sedona, filled with golf courses, hotels, friendly retirees, there was the red rock hill that I later found out is called Bell Rock and is home to the most visited trails leading to the major vortex sites. Bell Rock was right there, glowing in its red beauty surrounded by green trees, which I later found was Pinon and large Juniper trees that are native to Northern Arizona. Later, I have found out the mixture of green and red colors change the human mind to enhance mediumship abilities. Red color mostly focus on mental alertness, while green color stabilizes and elevates the mind on it inner conscious level. Therefore, the simple reason why traffic lights have the red light for a stop and the green light for to go. While we explore how this dance of colors has been significant in meditation and how it can helps build psychic ability and a direct mediumship with those that passed. Drive through the Bell Rock and the Courthouse area and take a look to the west side you will see one of the most iconic formations in the Southwest of the United States simply named Cathedral Rock, the home of not one, but two of the Sedona vortex sites. At this very location, you are now standing in the old sleeping volcano underneath you. This huge one million-year-old sleeping giant, has one big shaft, which opens to the surface of the Earth and makes Sedona big whirlpool geomagnetic vortex. When you ask the residents of Sedona where the vortex ley lines are located, most of them will reply that you are in the Vortex, Sedona itself is a giant vortex, which is invisible, but the sixth sense perceptive, some can feel its presence when driving. Sedona's red rock scenery put aside, the one could feel enrichment of human spirit and consequently, the whole body should be filled with the vortex energy. The second question many ask is why there is a vortex located under the Chapel of the Holy Cross, the answer could be found in the turbulent history of America. The Franciscan mission system had been established when the Southwest was the Spanish Royal territory and when the Sedona area location was the sacred place for the Indians before friars arrival. The missions such as; Santuario de Chimayo New Mexico, Santa Barbara California, San Xavier del Bac Tucson, have been established on the places of worship where the Natives gather before and it was the pattern that the new arriving religion would set their houses of worship on the already existing sacred sites. This attracted the converts to continue worship on the established places with a new twist in their spiritual lives. The friars had no clue that they would build their churches on the geomagnetic vortex, since the friars did not know that such geo phenomena is there. The native people knew that there is more into it, so they have etched thousands of petroglyphs spread throughout this region, which shows the spiral vortexes on the red stone with a clear description of their spiritual experience. The Ancient Native Americans of the Southwest were more sensitive to nature and had a special relationship to Mother Earth, which somehow lacks today. Some exceptions are always there, and one exception is Santuario de Chimayo in New Mexico, when old father Don Bernard, legend says, saw the image of illuminated silver cross on top of large hill above Chimayo Village, where later on, fr. Bernard decided to build his church down the creek, where is still standing to this day. On the road from the Oak Creek Village and over the Bell Rock area take a look to your right side and you notice the Chapel of the Holy Cross with its huge stained glass windows reflecting the sun lights. Road 89A leads to the Oak Creek bedrock and after the last roundabout, you will arrive at the bridge that is the center of the Gallery Row, where most of the Sedona art galleries are located. A few hundred yards in, before the Gallery Row Sedona's bridge, on the left bank of the Oak Creek there is less known vortex location, hidden Wind Tunnels. The road 89A climbs up for some hundred yards and will take you to the main intersection in Sedona where the Roads 179A and 89A meet and make the place called "Y". This is an unofficial center of Sedona and this is the spot where we can start our vortex hunting and a mediumship research. There are only two schools of thought in modern physics; the first is known to everyone and hold that the history's timeline goes in straight linear direction; the past, present, future as we know it. Second, is a quantum physics theory that sees time as we perceive it, just as an illusion, in which many of the events simultaneously flow in, in at least eleven dimensions, in which Julius Cesar and Napoleon fight their battles in different time or dimension. Whatever it may be the reality out of these two theories or even more of them, one is certain; we can tap in many different times with our inner minds or our souls. So many of those experiences of our past and the ones yet to happen, would roll down simultaneously in different dimensions, which can bridge space and time. Therefore, with meditations and prayers and with a huge help of Mother Earth we could bridge space and time, even reach future life experience not with our bodies, but with our minds. The people could experience clairvoyance, seeing past and future, while some will go a step more to achieve higher levels of psychic enhanced or medium experience talking to their loved ones recently passed with help of the Sedona vortexes that act as the antennas to the spiritual world. Almost everybody I have talked to could agree on one point; Sedona is the giant vortex, made of many more smaller vortexes in the Sedona area, the only question is, how many? The vortex maps that are available in many of Sedona stores, describe only the four most visited and the first discovered vortexes, however, you might discover one for yourself. One reason that this is the first vortexes found, is their very easy access from the paved roads and frequent visitations by hikers, so they made the easy way on the vortex map you have in your hands. These vortexes are; the Airport Mesa, Bell Rock, Red Rock Crossing, Cathedral Rock and Boynton Canyon. Cathedral Rock towers above Red Rock Crossing vortex that ends at the place called, the Buddha Beach. The vortex most visited and photographed is the Chapel of the Holy Cross. The Chapel is very easy to find and is open until five o'clock. The other two are, Fay Canyon and Schnebly Hill vortex. Last but not least, is the Indian Garden's Vortex, the very spot where the beautiful story of Sedona has begun. Jim Thompson's Indian Gardens are recently placed on the National Landmark list and are accessed with the highway 89A toward Flagstaff, next to the Sedona Fire Department in Oak Creek Canyon. Drive up the stream of Oak Creek Canyon, just before the switchbacks on the same road is location of the most hiked trail and least traveled vortex, is the West Fork Trail vortex. Another vortex less traveled, situated next to Palatki and recommended for medium work and solitary meditation is the Shaman's Cave vortex.

The story of Sedona

We will never find out when the story of Sedona started. It has been buried deep down in the Native American oral history and it could be summarized in the one advice the Native Americans of Northern Arizona gave me once: " If you are looking for what you are always looking for, you must go to Sedona!" What is known from modern history and what is taught to the visitors is that the story of Sedona begins with old pioneer called Jim Thompson. Traveling the stream of the Oak Canyon, pioneer Jim Thompson encountered the Native American settlement, which is today known as the Indian Gardens, and it is located about five miles up the stream in the Oak Canyon on the road 89A, the town northern exit toward Flagstaff. The first location is marked by large limestone with engraved bronze plaque commemorating this event and no note that the Indian Gardens is a hidden location of the vortex. Sedona's history of the last hundred and fifty years is very well documented, but if we dig deeper in the past, the picture becomes far more blurry. With new archeological evidence the presence of the first Paleo Indians was expected to be there, however, it was only in 1999 that the first material evidence is dug up in Honanki in form of the Clovis arrow's point. This find was only the start of rediscovering the Paleo history of Sedona that dates back to 11,500 to 9000 B.C. The presence of Paleo Indians in Sedona area is longer lasting than any other parts of the American Southwest either because of its milder climate or lush green fertile grounds around the Oak Creek and Beaver Creek area, which have attracted a large game which in turn is the main source of food for hunters or it could possibly be, the vortexes seducing geomagnetic energy, nowadays we can only speculate. Most of Sedona's Paleo-Indians have left the area of Sedona around 300 A.D., again we can only speculate why? Next period is described as the Archaic Period of the Verde Valley history and did last until the arrival of the first Sinagua, sometime around 600 A.D. The Archaic Period is far less known, since there is less than twenty percent of ground excavated.

Pueblos in History

The Sinagua ruins were well-known to the first pioneers occuping

Sedona in late 19th century, but an official American Archeology

was struggling for decades how to properly classify all the people

known as the "The missing ones". The Southwest Archeology was

in its early stages of development until 1920s. In early 1930s, the

archaeologists the American Southwest gathered in Pecos, invited

by Southwest archeology pioneer Adolph Kidder, so they decided

to standardize and to classify Paleo Indians of the Southwest. The

gatherings are still going on annually in various locations and are

part of ever-improving analysis of old data and discovering a new

one. Only about fifteen percent of all those estimated locations are

excavated, despite the years of professional work of the American

Archeologists on one side, with looters and treasure hunters on the

other side. The classification of the Pueblo Indians is concentrated

on the classic American Southwest that incorporates the states of

Arizona, New Mexico, Utah, Colorado and part of northern Mexico and from the very edges of Western Plains to the California's south. The old Southwest cultures are divided into the four major ones; the Hohokam Culture with center around modern town of Phoenix and Tucson to the south, and the north of the Verde Valley with Sedona as the center. The Mogollon Culture occupy the most southern New Mexico, extending to Verde Valley in southwest with the Mimbres the Salado subcultures within. The Patayan Culture is located from west of Sedona to California. Finally, the best-known culture for their architectural achievements was the Anasazi Culture with their territory that extends northeast of Sedona and Flagstaff, well into Colorado and Utah. The First Pecos Conference of the American Archeologists produced the first names for the great cultures of the Southwest: Hohokam, Patayan, Mogollon, and Anasazi. Old Pecos classification still stands today with some small changes in this one ever-evolving process. If the one take a look at historical borders of these cultures, the one will notice that they all border Sedona in the

Verde Valley area, but none of these are present on the large scale in the Sedona area. The problem began with a question of just how to classify Sinagua, which still persists today. The one major task for the American Archeologists was and is its timing of the Pueblo Culture, so the First Pecos conference has produced the framework for the timing of Pueblo evolution into our calendar (Cordell 1984). Pueblo time was divided as Basketmaker I, II, III, and Pueblo I, II, III, IV, V to fit the western historical time frame. Basketmaker I is defined as the Pre-agricultural society at the Pecos conference and replaced with the name Archaic (Cordell 1984). In Basketmaker II agriculture is present, pottery absent, and spear-thrower is used. In Basketmaker III, Pottery was present with decorative designs, with the agriculture present and with the cranial deformation of infants skulls is absent. The Cranial deformations were significant find in many cultures throughout the world. Archeology had one stepping stone in dividing the basket making history periods in the Pueblo society evolution in later Pueblo periods. The deformation found in the Southwest prompted the American archeology at a time to think that there are possibly two distinct ethnic groups among Puebloans. The First Pecos Conference of the American Archaeologists made the Pueblo classifications based on their burial items, architecture, and pottery. The Pueblo I period or the Proto Pueblo has some first evidence in cranial deformation in the skeletal remains. The villages were built high above the ground with their pit houses present, and the Pueblo building gets famous rectangular shape. The corrugated decorations are all present on most of the ceramics at top of vessels. The Pueblo II period is marked by small villages that often extend through the wider geographical areas, when Pueblo II pottery earns more outside plastic decorations. In Pueblo III period, the village becomes a town and this period is called the Classic Great Pueblo. In Pueblo IV the population declined, when the Great Pueblo was left for better soil and water, so many authors described this as the exodus from 1300's great drought. The Pueblo V is the period that is the most vivid in mind, because of the paintings from the earliest

Spanish Colonial occupation in which Pueblo gets known European elements and almost always, with the Church built on main square. This very idyllic picture of a classic pueblo village is what comes to mind and is very hard to imagine any other Pueblo that our eyes are not used to. Even those ruins of early settlements do not give up the secrets of the previous periods, which lay below the surface and the first impression that the ruin revealed to us. Another problem for a trained archeologist is that the mind wants to see linear evolution of the Pueblo's Village with the Pit-house building ends at the start of Pueblo's Village building. This is not the case and many of the Pit Houses continue to be built all the way to the twentieth century as temporary shelters. The transitions between the Pueblo's historical time periods are not very sharp and vary in time, from location to location. After the gradual decline in Chaco Canyon Culture, their famous masonry and pottery making skills moved south to Casas Grandes and north to Mesa Verde, way past 1300's.

Sinagua

Little is known about the history of this culture, since there are no oral or written records from their descendants. Sinagua left a large amount of evidence-based on their architectural ability, commonly known as the Pueblo structures, their arrival predates better-known culture to the North, the Anasazi. Sinagua name was adopted from the Spanish explorer who named the San Francisco Peaks as Sierra Sinagua (mountain without water), which is a great contrast to the truth, Flagstaff and Verde Valley is abundant with water. Harold S. Colton in 1939 is the first archaeologist who described Sinagua as culturally distinctive group from the Anasazi, Hohokam, Patayan, and Mogollon surrounded cultures that were distinctive from each other in masonry, pottery and weaving techniques. The archeology problem started to emerge on how to classify the ancient Sinagua. Since Sinagua have many cultural traits that were distinctive from all of the surrounding cultures, yet similar with each one of them, the one single question did arise; "Were Sinagua distinctive in their ethnicity and culture from the others, or were they just the melting pot"? Sinagua's inappropriate naming is just the first problem in the line of problems, which arise for emerging American Archaeology with questions; where Sinagua came from and to whom they were related and to which one of the nearby cultures; Hohokam, Patayan, Mogollon or Anasazi they most belong to. Many did point to Hopi tribe as their closest descendants, because of the Sinagua cultural similarity to Hopi. Western Pueblo today all share similar cultural and religious ties, which are summoned in its Kachina Cult and the Pre-Columbian cultures do not. Among today's surviving Western Pueblo tribes Hopi live in close proximity to the Ancient Sinagua territory and unlike Navajo and Apache, the Pueblo are sedentary Indians, not the nomads. Other fact is that the first nomadic tribes came to the area in the 1400s from Alaska and many other coastal regions of the American Northwest and even today the lower level of oral communication is possible between Apache Navajo and the

Native Americans of the American Northwest. Today, distant tribal members understand each other, and despite the fact that they were separated from each other for 600 years since the migration began. These problems come down to simple words, historicism, for many Europeans and the heritage for the Natives. Historicism does come from the 19th-century European philosophy led by the most famous German professor George Friedrich Wilhelm Hegel. Known for his Doctor's Club, George Hegel shaped the European philosophy and consequently, the American one. Finally, everything today is based on Hegel's philosophy, which has indirect influence on archeology. Historicism belief system is based on simple thesis that everything, which exists now is related to something in the past, for that reason should reappear in the future with different shape, but with similar essence. Therefore, history must repeat itself, its continuity should be present and in the Southwest that meant one culture continues to emerge from a previous one with its ethnic similarities. Hopi tribe should have had its direct link to Sinagua, just like Yuma and Pai tribes must have been the result of the Patayan Culture. With none of the living Anasazi descendants found today countless number of conspiracy theories about their disappearance have emerged. With not a trace of Anasazi present in archeology on the ground, the one explanation has been found with the exodus south to Mexico, even with the Alien abductions. We think of word continuity as the most crucial for our social existence or direction for the future. For most Native Puebloans this is far from the truth, since Navajo name for Anasazi translates in English quickly from the "Ancient Enemy" to the "Ancient Ancestors", just to satisfy the European mind need for matching Hegel's Historicism continuity. Edmund Burke once said that mankind history is the link between its dead, living and those yet to be born. This is a pretext for the classic Historicism that has arrived in the 19th century and if one mind does not match this way of the European thinking, we don't feel safe in the safety zone that we all grow up with. Sinagua is still a serious problem because all Sinagua's evidence does not fit in Historicism. Hegel's Historicism is passed down indirectly to most of the Native Puebloans, and is exactly how the Navajo word for the "Ancient Enemy" became the "Ancient Ones", only to lead with the new, the "Ancient Ancestor"! The other language translation fitting and adjustments are made to satisfy today's political correctness aggression which we are almost obsessed with. Used cars become the pre-owned vehicles and toilet paper becomes tissue, mankind becomes humankind. The scientific method in anthropology and archeology is subject to new political correctness and censorship. Clear evidence of cannibalism is found in the Anasazi Pueblos at the collapse of the Chaco Canyon Culture and it has always been downplayed or ignored just to satisfy current political correctness toward Navajo. Both Navajo and Apaches are nomadic people that have arrived at the scene of the Chaco Canyon history long after the Chaco Canyon Culture was gone and are not Puebloan tribes. In order to satisfy the European Historicism, most scientists turn to Puebloan Hopi, as their next best target, and living resource. Because Hopi participated in the Pueblo's Revolt against the Spanish Crown in 1680s and were excluded from Reconquest in the 1700s, most of the Hopi, Zuni and Acoma tribes were left alone and they became the true gem for many Anthropologists for staying culturally pristine and intact. Hopi has a very close connections to the Sinagua's religious ceremonies and rituals of the latter periods, the Kachinas, as many Pueblo tribes do. The ritual ceremonies and rain dances, with snake and Kachina dances are a common practice for Pueblos with the only exception of Taos Pueblo, where Kachina dance has been replaced with similar Turtle dance (Cordell 1984). On one of my visits to the Taos Pueblo I have found that half of the Red Willow tribe practice only Christianity, one fourth practice the syncretism of both Christian, and Pueblo tribal belief systems, and the last fourth reject anything that is of a "White man", they strictly adhere to the cultural and religious traditions. This is the historical, but also the "living culture" and so are the Hopi. On my visit to the Church of St. Jerome in the old Taos Village, it has been explained to me that the statue of Virgin is dressed up in special robes of four different colors depending on their seasons. Taos villagers dress up Mary's statue in the pink robe during spring equinoxes and the blue robe during summer solstices. Mary is dressed in the orange robe in the fall and during all winter solstices Mother Mary is dressed in the white robe. On my question why is that, the tribal representative has explained that in the course of Tewa history, Mary was made in the embodiment of Mother Earth Deity, which Red Willow worshiped before. Mother Earth's colors changed from pink in spring, blue in summer, its fall color is orange and snow-white in winter. This is a classic example of the religious syncretism imposed on Puebloans, after 400 years of western pressure. Most of Western Pueblos were spared from the Inquisition reach and gold grabbing Anglos, who just focused on exterminating Sue from the Black Hills and many of California tribes during the last California's Gold Rush. I have been taken to the old crime scene from the 1850s, the Old Church of Taos Pueblo, which is now in ruins. Some two hundred women and children together with the Friars were taken to the Church and burnt alive by arriving Anglos and my guide told me: "You see Sir, the Spaniards were not that bad!" After many years of the Spanish imposed oppression, the eastern Pueblos in the Rio Grande Valley kept their dances and religious ceremonies in secret and to this day there are no known public ceremonies in place. In contrast, most of Western Pueblos; Hopi, Zuni, Acoma, and Laguna are always very visual, and proud of their Kachina dances and their annual festivals are open to the public. No evidence ever existed that either cultures were related, but they interacted through the trade. It is well-known that the Chaco flourish sometimes between 900-1150 and that was abandoned around 1150 A.D. starting with the drought around year 1130. The Chaco Canyon Culture is located in the place with a very little spring water supply that cann't sustain neither wildlife nor the agriculture, in contrast to the Sedona area, where the Verde Valley water streams and creeks are more than plentiful coming from the snow covered San Francisco Peaks. Despite the worst drought ever recorded by tree ring dating, the San Francisco Peaks is the largest basin of underground waters in the American Southwest. For that one reason, the long droughts could not be the only explanation for Sinagua's sudden overnight disappearance, possible violent warfare with the arriving Athabascan tribes, might. Archeological evidence of possible warfare in Sedona or other violent ending like a natural disaster does not exist. The Four Corners area has its very strong evidence of longest drought in 1300s, followed by warfare, human ritual sacrifice, cannibalism, with none of this pretends to Sinagua. Sinagua finally, simply vanished without a trace by year 1400 A.D. Sinagua should have survived the droughts in the area, researchers believe Sinagua moved to the north with no explanation, why? In 1300 A.D., Yavapai moved to Sedona, followed by Apache in 1400 A.D., when the last Sinagua were still present. The first of Yavapai were semi-nomadic and hunter-gatherer, like the Apache that came after and they did not build the high Pueblo structures or elaborate irrigation systems like Sinagua. Why Sinagua left and what really happened to them, is their mystery bigger than Anasazi one. Hopi claim their ancestry to Sinagua like all Zuni and Navajo claim their link to Anasazi despite their name Anasazi, which means in Navajo "The ancient enemy". The most recent translationd and much more acceptable for us and most the Natives in the area is, "The Ancient Ones." Most of the American anthropologists believe that none of the present Pueblo descended from Anasazi and all recent research points that Anasazi were driven out by the Aztec related clans from Mexico that have infiltrated the Chaco culture, tried to reshape the cultural and religious beliefs, which with the great drought present has resulted in violent end for the Chacoans. None of this applies to Sinagua, no drought, warfare, or any large merge in hundred years of their long-lasting coexistence with the Yavapai tribe in the area. Found to be far more mysterious is the origin of Southern Sinagua. It has been proven that Sinagua came to the area in 600 A.D., and that their arrival on the scene of history is always judged by all the archeological evidence found on the ground. Most of the Puebloan town-building periods are expected to be predated by the pit-house building periods, just as the ceramic pottery periods are predated by the basket making periods in the Sinagua history. Some researchers date the earliest known Sinagua presence as early as 300- 400 A.D. Everybody in the archeology community should agree on 600 A.D. Sinagua in early period built rounded pit houses, which were small with entrances from their roofs and Sinagua were hunter-gatherers and a significant amount of the material evidence was dug out from Montezuma Castle and just recently from Honanki all point out that the agricultural and community structure of the Southern Sinagua's society begins gradually. The first known archeological period of the Sinagua presence and the first evidence of single pit houses are found in the Pueblo archeology as early as the Pueblo I period that is associated with basket making. The Pueblo II period is followed by the first known appearance of the ceramics and with their larger number of the pit housing units. Pueblo III is what we could see in most of the Verde Valley area including the area of Sedona where a small village had big aspirations of becoming a small town, where they would interact with a whole net of the surrounding Sinagua's communities in larger organized social structure. It was in the year 900 A.D., when the cultural features of Sinagua formed that could culturally separate them from surrounding cultures from Prescott to the west, Anasazi to the north, and Hohokam to the south Phoenix and Tucson areas. This big cultural difference has been followed in the distinctive ceramics that are redware reflect Sedona soil and are of better quality than the gray-black pottery of the Prescott culture. The Sinagua redware clay ceramics are not of extraordinary quality compared with the Hohokam Culture to the south, however, that is very distinctive in beautiful patterns. Sinagua red-brown pottery is all different from the White Mountain pottery of the same period in the 1250-1275 A.D., which is also redware but with some different color patterns. This could be the small influence that came from the trade since Sinagua was at its cultural influence peak around years 1250-1275 A.D. The Pottery was traded and exchanged throughout Southwest history, but it is not the case with the Sinagua's southern neighbors. There were no contacts with the Salado Culture that was contemporary with Sinagua and none of Salado pottery was found anywhere in the Verde Valley. There are no Salado pottery found in Honanki or Palatki sites nor any other Southern Sinagua site, which archeologists describe as the Honanki period, or in the later period, like the Montezuma Castle or Tuzigoot National Monument towns that are marked as the Tuzigoot period, which is at Sinagua sunset in 1300-1400 A.D. The basket making craft is another feature with which we could trace the Sinagua culture to a lesser extent since the Pueblo II basket making period is shared with the intercultural trade from when it has begun, and even to the Hopi basket making that is almost identical with smaller yucca treads. Sinagua basket craft was the same throughout centuries, and their treads were similar to their surrounding cultures, and all point out that the initial craft of basket making was learned in immemorial past and we can trace Sinagua basket making period as the next period, following early pit-houses building periods. The Sinagua pit-houses that were built around the year 600 A.D. were small, rounded with the circular long entryway. The Sinagua houses changed most of their shapes around 900 A.D. when they become more rectangular with the four marking points. The Sinagua houses of this period have many cultural features that connect them to neighbors like significant ante-chamber, and with the peripheral post patterns and the signs of burial cremation point toward the trade with surrounding cultures. The jewelry found in this period has many beautiful seashell beads attached, which tells us that the trade will go as far as the Sea of Cortez and even inland into Mexico. Sinagua late period falls in the Pueblo III period that all American Archeologists pick as period which still includes their pit houses built, as most Sinagua villages become the small towns, the weaving technology present and finally with the introduction of the Kachina concepts as their first common religion. The Kachina concepts in the Tuzigoot phase of the Southern Sinagua falls in the Pueblo IV, which we could see in the Tuzigoot and in Montezuma Castle. The experts in the weaving techniques point that Sinagua's multicolor techniques are very visible in today's Hopi blankets. The Southern Sinagua village was tenfold smaller than impressive towns of; Chaco, Aztec or Cortez to the North. The Chaco Culture used to have more than 800 rooms, the Mesa Verde 200 plus, the Honanki, Palatki, Montezuma Castle, even Tuzigoot have on average, 25-30 rooms with no rounded Kivas found anywhere and there is always community room at the far end of their Village present. The Hopi's oral tradition holds that all the Hopi clans came from the South and those, which went westward were never heard from again and those which went further south were all slaughtered and Hopi that moved to the north are those Hopi that do populate the Hopi Mesas today. The Hopi Water Clan claims their ancestors came from the south of what is the Hopi reservation today. The end of the story close with surviving Sinagua move to the Hopi Mesas and merge with Hopi. With no other explanation, so far, this concept of the last survivors of the late Southern Sinagua is still the most acceptable one. People simply do not disappear and someone always survive.

Sinagua the Ancient Americans

Sinagua were occupying Verde Valley with Sedona as its spiritual center which does correspond to the Hopi legend of the lost city of Palatkwapi with it certain location, which matches the ancient ruin of Palatki, which is the short form of Palatkwapi (Pinkham 2012). Palatki is the site of many petroglyphs made by Sinagua, but also the Paleo-Indians and the Archaic Indians prior to the Yavapai, and Sinagua habitation. The Zuni tribe has a legend which is associated with the Sedona origins. These few remnants of the modern Pueblo oral history supports Peter Pilles theory, in which the last Sinagua merged with modern the Hopi and Zuni tribes, and were adopted as an ancient refugees. From what or whom Sinagua were running we would probably never find, but the one prevalent theory among the archaeologists and anthropologists today does not exist. Many of the previous theories were circulating around all these major ideas. Sinagua moved somewhere else because of the disease or drought.

The Verde Valley area has never been subject to droughts since an abundance of the waters coming from the tops of the San Francisco Peaks had been always supplying Oak Creek, Wet and Dry Beaver Creeks in Sedona. There is no existing evidence of warfare or any other violent end, that is a far cry from the Chaco Canyon Culture's cannibalism evidence. Even if the superb agricultural and irrigation systems, which classic Sinagua develop at Montezuma Castle and Montezuma Well collapsed, there were still plenty of those hunting and gathering resources in the green valley. Peter Pilles points out, there was no reason to move to the dry Hopi Mesas and at least not the entire community. The second theory that was proposed in the past was that there was a violent end. There is no clear evidence of any warfare or fire in any known archeological site so far. The third theory was built on the simple idea that Sinagua are entirely Hopi. There is again, not even a trace of any archaeological evidence that modern or ancient Hopi ever occupied the Honanki and the Palatki sites as Yavapai and Apache did after 1400. The most likely answer

exist today is the most prevalent theory that the surviving Sinagua

merged with Hopi and Zuni tribe and in Verde Valley with Yavapai

tribe. This same pattern is here with the modern Americans of their

last 250 years. Sinagua were distinctive enough to be unique culture

in their own right, and since Sinagua were situated in this "melting

pot" of the entire American Southwest, with most elements of all

the neighboring cultures, fight for Sinagua cultural independence is

still going on, among the American anthropologists-archaeologists

alike. Both Salado and Mimbres were in a more favorable position

and because the main question of the Salado Culture is; how is the

Salado Culture related to the Hohokam Culture and in the Mimbres

case how much and if the Mimbres Culture is related to Mogollon.

The Salado Culture is geographically positioned between Hohokam

to the west, Mogollon to their east, and Anasazi to the north. Salado

were the superb master pottery craftsmen, and extensively trade the

pottery with everybody around, except for Sinagua bordering them

to their northwest. Mimbres were the most famous among Ancient

Puebloans when it comes to their superb animal effigy images in an art of pottery making. In fact, when the first Mimbres pottery were excavated, many archeologists believed that it was the work of the contemporary artist, at first. The Mimbres and Salado Cultures are believed to be more separate cultures, based just on their distinctive ceramics alone, and it was very hard to place them within any other culture around as their inner subgroup. Mimbres had one advantage, which is their unique burial ritual. Most of the Mimbres pottery are found with a little hole drilled in the middle of them, and the dishes were placed over the faces of their deceased, allowing their souls to pass to the underworld. The dishes were mostly painted with their spirit animal that is apotheosis of their soul passing or making one's soul godlike or in which their guardian spirit accompanies the soul to the afterlife. In the Sinagua case, the question was how Sinagua fit the other Ancient Pueblo cultures.

Sinagua and Hohokam

Attempt to make Sinagua part of the Hohokam culture was made in the early sixties when the cultural term Hakataya had been coined, refer to the broad Hohokam of the larger Phoenix and Tucson areas that were related to their ethnic territory to the south but spread out in their cultural terms to the larger Arizona area (Schroeder 1960). The proposal which would include the Sinagua Culture in this area was rejected. The archeologists who wanted to see Sinagua as part or offshoot of the larger Hohokam culture based their intention on only two material finds, as the evidence found in the large Sinagua Homeland. First were small Ball Court fields found in the Sinagua territory that were very similar to those Hohokam Ball Court fields found throughout Phoenix, and Tucson. This Ball game was very popular throughout all territories of a larger Mesoamerican World, and was internationally popular. The ancient game is found in the most of Mayan and Aztec cities and one Hohokam well-preserved is located in Snaketown Arizona. The second hard evidence of the Hohokam culture is the single Pithouse found in Winona Village, which is much different from any of Sinagua pit houses ever found which includes the rest of the pit houses to the north toward Winona Village. Dr. Peter Pilles believes that this single pit house has all the features of the classic Hohokam village, and was the pit house built by the trader who lived in the north Sinagua country, the trade and diplomat at the same time. It is well-known that these cultures were trading between each other, especially sought Mesoamerican items, such as the colorful Macaw feathers and royal blue tie-dyed textiles. Other than the ball court and the single pit house that is found, there were no other Hohokam features found in the Sinagua area, so far. The small trading items such as pottery are not enough evidence of the Hohokam habitation or large coming migrant population south from the Phoenix area. Even the greater Phoenix irrigation systems which are the hallmark of Hohokam's sophisticated agriculture are nowhere to be found in Sinagua territory. The best-built irrigation canal system is still visible at Montezuma Castle and Montezuma Well, and they are a far cry from the sophistication of the Hohokam agricultural system. With expansion of the residential areas around Phoenix, Yuma, and Tucson, the irrigation systems are now almost everywhere excavated. Another problem to link the Sinagua and the Hohokam cultures, is the Salado culture, halfway between Phoenix and Sedona. The Salado culture is one more clear example of their cultural denial , like in the Sinagua's case. Salado is still disputed as independent culture, and archeology today questions can Salado be the independent culture that is based on their unique pottery alone. The old school of thought holds that the Salado is a very distinctive culture from all the others based only on their pottery. Both Salado and Mimbres pottery are the most beautiful polychrome pottery and sought after by collectors and poachers alike. The irony is that both Salado and Mimbres pottery artists are found to be the most famous pottery artists in entire American Art history, rivaling any modern artists, as they face their cultural denial. Salado is often viewed just as an offshoot of larger Hohokam Culture and Mimbres as a part of the Mogollon Culture. The Salado lands encompasses Sedona to the southern end of Verde Valley, and to the northern part of what are nowadays Phoenix areas. Both Sinagua and Hohokam shared the same neighbor in between and that is Salado, which place Salado as the additional territorial boundary between Sinagua and Hohokam. It is very interesting that there were no Salado items ever excavated in any of the Sinagua towns and villages, despite the fact of Salado being the most beautiful polychrome pottery found in the American Southwest. It looks like the first door neighbors Salado and Sinagua did not talk to each other. There was not a single evidence of fight, warfare or natural distraction, but despite the fact that Salado and Sinagua were separated by a small mountain, there was no trade for all those centuries. On the other hand, both Sinagua and Hohokam were trading heavily, however not enough to overpower each other cultures. The name Hohokam comes from Pima language where the Hohokam singular means the one that left or is gone (Haury 1976).

Thus, the Hohokam are, "those who are gone" or "who vanished",
and this indicates the ancestors of modern Pima tribe had a warfare
connection with the old Hohokam. Pima's oral history points to their
final battle with last known Hohokam, which resulted in Hohokam
ultimate defeat most likely, their extermination. The Great Pueblo is
an outdoor museum in the heart of Phoenix that holds the evidence
of this Great Pueblo abandonment, even before the Spanish arrival.
Salado cultural denial and difference from the Hohokam Culture
are only based on magnificent pottery, where the other aspects of
Salado are deemed to be more similar, if not the same to Hohokam,
including their architecture, clothing, and basket making. Sinagua,
on the other hand, have more material evidence that makes Sinagua
unique independent culture, even the separate ethnic group, yet the
Sinagua culture is shadowed by their denial that seems to continue.

Sinagua and Patayan

Sinagua western neighbors in the same time period of their history are Patayan. The Hualapai word Patayan, means "the old people". Patayan are the ancestors of the Yuman tribe. The Yuman tribes are well aware of their ancestral lineage to Patayan, with no historical disconnect with this case. Yuman people nowadays occupy most of western Arizona are diversified physically and linguistically, as the Quechan, Cocopah, Mojave, Walapai, Yavapai, Maricopas, Yuma. In Pre-Columbian time the Patayan Culture extended to California, Baja California, and to the Colorado River in the south, north from Kingman all the way to the Grand Canyon. These Patayan cultural traditions include the Prescott and the Cerbat Branches and the two were immediate neighbors to Sinagua, the Patayan culture is mostly found west of the ghost town of Jerome. The Patayan Culture was hunter based throughout their history with limited agriculture. The Patayan agriculture is described as flood harvesting agriculture and was not as sophisticated as Sinagua in Verde River Valley. Little of architectural evidence was found to support social structure, but the great amount of the Patayan pottery was found which easily helps to identify this culture. Most of the Prescott Patayan pottery are plain, never corrugated like in the later periods and Patayan pottery is the most famous for Black-on-Gray often called Prescott Gray. The San Francisco Mountain Grayware is often found between Kingman and Grand Canyon. One characteristic that is similar to Sinagua are the rectangular community rooms that are found on the eastern end of the village. Pilles strongly believe that this community room served for ceremonial and religious practices. The great rounded Kiva or the big house found in the Anasazi areas is always missing, and one community room is always rectangular and never in the center of their habitation. The Patayan houses were surface longhouses and shallow pit houses always with very small community rooms at the end of a village, missing in the later periods of Patayan history and can only suggest the social change. The small community room at the end of their village was missing in those later historical periods and could be used for storage as archaeologists suggest or points out to the lack of food supplies for the following year. The Community Room was used for ceremonial and religious purposes that made a social change in regard to the Patayan beliefs. Patayan, did survive their Sinagua neighbors that left Verde Valley in the 1400s, and the last archeological evidence points out to the year 1550 A.D. Unlike Sinagua in the Tuzigoot phase which based their economic survival entirely on sophisticated agriculture with the gravitational irrigation system at the Montezuma Well and Montezuma Castle, the Patayan Culture was a hunter-gatherer based with some seasonal agriculture present. The Patayan culture was more resistant to the possibility of droughts and warfare. This is another reason to question Sinagua's rapid disappearance since the archeological evidence of a drought, warfare, and disease are missing. More American anthropologists hypothesize the religious reason for the surviving Sinagua move to the Hopi Mesas. This is a puzzle since most of Southwest Pueblo cultures shared the same Kachina cult and/or rain dances, since the Kachina Cult was introduced first by Hopi, after late 1300s, when Sinagua has been in a major decline. Did some retreating Sinagua refugees bring their new religion to the Hopi Mesas with them? Excavations of "the priest burial" site at Anderson Mesa where the last Sinagua retreated and the Tuzigoot priest burial may suggest so. After 1300 A.D. the congregation of Sinagua occurs at the Tuzigoot for Southern Sinagua, and up at Anderson Mesa and the Chaves Pass for Northern Sinagua. The general rule is; their towns become too big and their position on the elevated ground must suggest more defensive organization of their society. The smaller dwellings were abandoned and the population shows their move toward the higher grounds, and to the more defensive structures.

Sinagua and Mogollon

The Pioneer archeologist Harold Colton viewed Sinagua as a part of the large Mogollon tradition, McGregor saw Sinagua more Patayan, and others view Salado, Mimbres, and Sinagua cultures as divisions among one Mogollon culture, which includes most of east Arizona. Today this view is mostly changed in favor of the old southwestern cultures as separate and distinctive cultures. The Mogollon territory extended North from Little Colorado River where they met Anasazi of New Mexico. East edge of the Mogollon territories was situated from the Guadalupe Mountain chain in eastern New Mexico, all the way to Verde Valley where Mogollon met Sinagua. Unlike Sinagua whose first records in the Sedona area started as early as 600 A.D., and Mogollon start as early as 200 A.D., with their first attempt of agriculture and pottery making (Cordell, 1984). The big Mogollon territory was favorable for hunting big game, and like in the case of Patayan, Mogollon tradition survived the drought of 1300 and even became a sanctuary for the Anasazi refugees. The population crash was seen as the migrations in the Southwest, with the last surviving Sinagua going to the Hopi Mesas or even disappearing altogether. The ancient Mogollon tradition have a few phases in development, it start sometime in years 550-950 A.D. and is marked as the period of a great stability in the region with the Mogollon agriculture and their pottery started, and a hunting-gathering practice remains as an important activity for Mogollon which endured in their culture for the next millennia. The pottery remains mostly plain red-brown and with red overlay similar to those early Sinagua. Later on, there was decoration on the pottery found in red color, houses are arranged as small villages, believed to be built for Mogollon extended families. This cultural landscape for Mogollon persists for the next 400 years until their next phase. The Anasazi so called, the "Take over" phase of the Mogollon Culture growth as it was seen by the Archeologists takes place between 950-1150 A. D. The Mogollon round dwelling, which is partially below ground are persistent for the entire period, however, the Anasazi rectangular Pueblo's building is for the first time built with the central community Plaza in the Anasazi village, which is not the case with Sinagua. Archeologists believe that this was the Anasazi's occupation of large Mogollon territory, however, there is no evidence of fire and violence. Mogollon adopted all the Anasazi's new trends in architecture and ceramics. It is possible but not plausible for this to happen "overnight". Southern Sinagua and even their north branch in the Flagstaff area were not even affected, in contrast, the Sinagua culture flourishes at this time. Puzzling fact is just why the population of the larger cultures such as; Hohokam, Mogollon, or Anasazi never took control of neither the Sinagua nor the Patayan tradition. During the Pueblo III phase in some dramatic change around 1150 -1350 A.D. which affected the Southwest, with the archeological evidence of migrations, population collapse, fire, and drought, Sinagua were not affected. In contrast, Sinagua were in the middle of their cultural and population expansions during the Honanki and Palatki phases in their history. This is the time when the famous legend of the Sinagua's Red city Palatkwapi originated, Palatkwapi means "the Red City" and the term "Palatki" is a short form of it, which means the Red House (Pinkham 2012). The Hopi legend says that the city is located north of the Hopi Mesas and this must be Sedona. Francisco Coronado's famous historic Palatkwapi Trailhead leads westward toward the Sedona area. Most Northern American tribes have the same narrative for the origin of the souls in "Sipapu", which is an underground. Sinagua Sipapu is certainly located around the Wupatki National Monument, almost eighteen miles north from Flagstaff, where the whole underground cavern is present with openings that make the blowing wind sound, based on the thermal-air difference of the outside temperature of the air and the air trapped in the caverns. That small fissure like opening in the ground makes the cold air blowing from below, up in hot summers when the temperatures can rise in the hundreds within a few hours, forcing the cold air to blow up due to air temperature difference.

Sinagua and Anasazi

Sinagua that lived on those edges of the Anasazi's territory, notably the Sinagua northeastern branches of what is today's Flagstaff, must have had at least some interactions with Anasazi, however, Sinagua archeological evidence never shows, "the takeover". The Mogollon case shows some change, and whether the last of Anasazi moved to Mogollon area as the traders, conquerors, or just refugees. Anasazi changed the shape of Mogollon architecture and ceramics past 1000 A.D. In the case of Southern Sinagua the presence of broad Anasazi cultural influences are only limited to small items such as pottery, and there is numerous evidence of sought after Mesoamerican trade items, Macaw feathers and tie-dyed indigo clothing (Pilles 1984). Anasazi territory is the vast area east of Little Colorado River and includes all the surrounding territories in the "Four Corners" area, which includes the whole of New Mexico, Utah, Colorado, and all of Arizona. Since the First Pecos Classification was established, the

Anasazi Culture has been seen as the single distinctive culture with branches named; the Chaco Canyon, Mesa Verde, Rio Grande, and Virgin- Kayenta branch, based on the architectural features and the ceramic evidence. In the 1970s, the "Chaco Canyon Phenomena" term was coined, which includes the most sophisticated Culture in North America, and this would drive an enormous influence on the American Southwest and Continent through the trade (Lexon 1984). Today, the debate is going on between mainstream archaeologists and anthropologists was the Anasazi Culture one unique, domestic culture originated in the Southwest, as vast majority now believe, it was the culture which migrated from Mesoamerica as the branch of the large Aztec Culture. It is interesting to note that both Hopi and Papago are linguistically related to the Aztec Language group. The Chaco Phenomenon term is accepted, and is now widely used, which describes almost impossible building techniques in such arid climate with lack of water and without the horses, wheels or cattle that were brought much later by the Spanish. It seems that the first Anasazi arrived in the Four Corners area some time in the unknown past and brought their Aztec culture to the Southwest in the form of masonry, pottery, basketry, but even more important, the peace and social order in the entire Southwest. According to pioneer Professor Christy Turner, at Arizona State University, warfare was present in the archeological evidence dating back to 900 A.D., unexpectedly the archeological evidence of warfare comes to a sudden end in the Southwest. Prof. Christy Turner proposed that the first arrival of the Aztec Culture known as Anasazi corresponds to the first 250 years of peace and social order in the entire Southwest. Anasazi left most of the evidence of trade with Patayan in the form of pottery sold to Patayan, primarily from those Kayenta-Virgin branches of Anasazi, present in most of the archeological evidence found in the Kingman and Prescott areas. Furthermore, the famous Prescott gray on white pottery found in the Patayan area, which Dr. Harold Colton coined as unique to the Prescott areas are influenced by both Kayenta and

Virgin branches of Anasazi which were geographically more close to Prescott and Kingman. Sinagua sites in the Sedona area are also found to have the Anasazi pottery, that is always characteristically black on white which indicate that the trade was still going on with Anasazi, and was absent with the Salado Culture, which was more geographically close to Sedona Sinagua. Another influence of this new Mesoamerican cult which arrived at the historical scene of the American Southwest can be seen in the most Sinagua ruins with the presence of ceremonial objects, like were the macaw's feathers and Mesoamerican royalty clothing objects in form of indigo blue dyed pieces found in Honanki Heritage site. In 1977 prof. dr. Ana Sofaer found in the Chaco Canyon Culture, on the site called Fajada Butte, which is mesa overlooking the famous Anasazi system of religious temples, and the very complex system of timekeeping. For the next twenty years famous art historian, Ana Soafer introduced her new project called the "The Solstice Project", that yield this fascinating time and astronomy monitor of the Sun movement. The obsession with this solar timekeeping could be traced to the religious cults in Mesoamerica with their contemporary culture. In the Chaco Canyon Fajada Butte, the three boulder slabs were found overlying the large spiral circles carved in the giant rock slabs, so the site has been then coined, "The Sun Dagger". Surely and precisely at every sunset, on every summer solstice, sunrays appear through their precise target position, and it hit the spiral circle right in the middle. The Sunrise light during every winter solstice shows sunrays that appear at the end of every spiral circle and during the fall and the spring equinox, the sun rays would appear to be perpendicular to each other. These timekeeping clocks are found on the Sinagua sites, particularly on Northern Sinagua sites, such as, the Wupatki National Monument Mesas, and the etched spirals were also found at Sedona's Honanki and at the V-Bar-V. The spiral can be associated with the migration movement of the Hopi social group and today is believed that they had more astronomical, time recording or vortex location purposes. It is also very important to note that on some Sinagua petroglyphs are vividly carved spiral circles with the rays on the outside of the spirals, which clearly could point toward the vortex representation. The Southern Sinagua spiral lacks the Sun slabs above the spirals to function as the sun clock and the spirals missing the sun rays, which is carved on the spiral outskirts, it can be even possible that some of them do represent the vortices in the area. The four main elements in all the Native American cultures are; air, water, dirt, wind, so the spiral could well represent the famous slogan; "As above so below". Northern Sinagua Mesas and Wupatki National Monument border Anasazi's homeland and their timekeeping influence is also present. Another feature is the "ballcourt" that is built not only in Sinagua's sites but also in the Hohokam land, Phoenix and Tucson areas. It is particularly fascinating the ballcourt in Snaketown Arizona, which can hold more than two thousand spectators. The Ball Courts were built throughout Mesoamerica and are associated with the religious practice of ritual sacrifice. Neither violence nor ritual sacrifice are found in Sinagua of Verde Valley nor at any other known Northern

Sinagua sites. While Sinagua adopted most of the fashion, pottery, and various other trade items from their contemporaries, there is no evidence that Sinagua adopted the sacrificial rituals or cannibal cult found by Prof. Christy Turner in the Chaco Canyon Culture that is a hallmark of their Aztec Mesoamerican religion. It is known that the rounded Kivas were inner centers of the Anasazi religious and daily ceremonial practice, and rounded Kivas are found throughout their Anasazi homeland and later on in the Mogollon land at the Wupatki Mesas. It is now more clear why Hopi did choose their mesas on the higher ground with a little running stream water, where scarce water is collected in the few seasonal washes and the irrigation collecting systems. The Mogollon Culture seems to be taken over by retreating Anasazi since the final Anasazi migration has extended all the way south to the Casas Grande and even further, deep down to Mexico. The Patayan Culture somehow survived violence and was present in the area until the Spanish conquest. Sinagua that survived moved to the Hopi Mesas and some might have joined the incoming Yavapai-

Apache who lived with Sedona Sinagua from 1300-1400. In 1300, Anasazi major cultural center, the Chaco Canyon Culture was in serious decline. The great drought in 1276-1299 A.D. caused the final collapse of the Mesoamerican cannibal cult that ran Anasazi for more then two hundred years. The Chaco Culture final collapse pushed Anasazi to build new towns to the north of Chaco Canyon, which is today known as the Aztec and the Salmon Ruins. The last center of the Anasazi culture has been moved further north to Mesa Verde, and south to Casas Grandes via the Mogollon territory. It is known through the pottery evidence that Anasazi merged with the Casas Grandes population, however, the whereabouts of the Mesa Verde population is still unknown. It has been reported that persons went missing in the Mesa Verde National Park, and some tv crews, and amateur physicists are working on the possible time lapse and time portal presence investigation at Mesa Verde National Park.

The Tuzigoot Phase

Tuzigoot was not called by this name when the excavation began in 1933. Tuzigoot in Apache language means, "The Crooked Water", named after a lake near the city of Clarkdale. It can be reached from highway 89a coming from Prescott or Sedona. The name for the site excavation was the suggestion of Earl Jackson, Montezuma Castle custodian in the year 1933. Tuzigoot big dig was both the fortunate and unfortunate undertaking in harsh times of the Great Depression. Fortunately, because no such large dig on this scale has been taken, before or after the Great Depression in Arizona, or any surrounding states. Tuzigoot dig was funded by federal money, which is strange considering this unfortunate time of the Great Depression and there was nothing beneficiary for the society in terms of their immediate money turn around, like in the case of Hoover Dam, for example. On the other hand, President Franklin D. Roosevelt welcomed any great projects that would provide the jobs and judgment at that time was, that any of the archeological digs on this scale would provide immediate jobs, as well as, promote tourism in Arizona. Tuzigoot excavation was the major fiasco, an unfortunate one, according to some because it was done very quickly with the guidance of two undergraduate students, Edward Spicer and Louis Caywood, with their crew of 48 men, which had no formal training in archeology, and with the small crew of pottery's lab women with no training in archeology as well. Despite the facts, an extraordinarily great job had been done for that Era, in a record short time. The boys were very lucky since the dig was owned by the local mining company, which provided their mining equipment, and even their laboratory expertise. The ancient roads led through the Winslow Arizona area, with one road, which leads to the Northern Sinagua sites, and the major road leading to the Verde Valley and Prescott area. The final stage of Tuzigoot masonry was no match for the Anasazi masonry quality, however, it is better than Patayan in the Prescott area, and at least, have the dramatic design, more striking than the Hohokam

Culture of the Phoenix basin. The clay is red, which matches the iron-rich Sedona red rocks but of poor quality and the 1930s crew did much reconstruction. The major differences in the Honanki's building style and Tuzigoot is the entrance from their houses roof. Archeologist Todd Bostwick believes that this is for the defensive reason since can't definitely be for the practical one. With none of the ventilation shafts, all the smoke from cooking and heating must make Sinagua's everyday life miserable. Anthropologists still don't know much about the Sinagua's religion at the time, but Tuzigoot reveals an extraordinary amount of evidence that points to the very different form of ceremonies and rituals, which put them apart from the Anasazi ones, and their absence of the ritual sacrifice. Just like in the case of Prescott Patayan rounded Kiva is never found, rather there is a community room, which Peter Pilles and Todd Bostwick attribute to their rituals and ceremonies. The community room has unusual, hard to explain post holes, that both Bostwick and Pilles believe are some leftovers from the altar, room #4 has an elevated floor slab, one of the rooms in the center of town, is rectangular and has ritual linked items, such as the obsidian with chalcedony flakes, azurite, and malachite stones. The community rooms are associated with their religion and twelve adult graves are found, with children graves left under their parent's room floors. The children, therefore, had not been fully ready for the afterlife, and were left secured deep down under the family's home to be guarded by their parents in the afterlife (Bostwick). There were more than four hundred Sinagua's graves excavated in Tuzigoot, and the dead continue to speak about their lives and passage to the afterlife. All graves were covered with wooden poles, the adults were oriented north-south, and unlike the Anasazi bodies that were aligned always toward the east? It is very important to note that at the Anasazi gravesites, only those Anasazi bodies were buried with uttermost reverence and respect for resting Anasazi dead; the bones of victims of their sacrificial rituals, were desecrated with no order nor respect and were dumped in the mass graves. The Anasazi victim's skulls were crack open on both sides behind the ear lines, so the number of skulls could be "bead up" in lines, like the rosary beads. This is done, just like in Mesoamerica, so that the living are terrified daily and the social order is enforced. In addition, some of those skulls were cracked open from the neck side, so that the skulls can be posted on the poles in their Temples. Sinagua religion, on the other hand, had a great reverence for their bodies and the bodies were accompanied by the ceremonial objects. Jewelry found honors the Sinagua dead at Tuzigoot; with bracelets, amulets, beads, small pearl pendants figurines, especially for their children. The Children's graves were covered with the stone slabs unlike adult graves which were mostly covered with wooden poles, probably for their children's protection. The bodies were aligned in two different position arrangements in regard to their genders. The Man's bodies were always aligned with the head north-south, while the women's bodies were aligned in south-north alignment. What is the real reason for this, we can only speculate, but this contributes to the evidence of Sinagua's very distinctive religion? The pottery buried with Sinagua dead accompanied only less than one-third of their dead, unlike in all other Southwestern burial sites, which does point out to very different religious practices. Since Sinagua's dead did not need any water or any of the material terms in the afterlife, pottery has to have a more decorative purpose and was reserved for the higher social status of the deceased. Sinagua will drink from the spiritual waters in the afterlife. Another very important aspect of the Sinagua's religion, prior to the start of Kachina cult is, according to Todd Bostwick, presence of the social material justice for the dead. Socially highly positioned individuals did not carry much material goods in the afterlife, and everybody will get one piece of pottery. There is almost always an exception to the rule, and Tuzigoot does have an exception, and the very significant one, called "The Priest burial", and is the only grave found with extraordinary amounts of burial gifts for journey to the afterlife, with exceptionally beautiful items ever found in Sinagua gravesites. The priest's body is unique for the Sinagua burials due to the ceremonial beads around his left wrist are all red, while the ceremonial beads around his right wrist are in black color. This is precisely how the colors are displayed in the Kachina religion even today, and this is universal throughout the Southwest. That would imply, that this burial is a very late Sinagua, with the buried priest of the transitional Kachina Cult. Most of these archeology facts on the ground suggest that Sinagua have accepted the Kachina religion even before leaving the Valley. Since Hopi are credited with origins of the Kachina Cult this would put the Sinagua refugees fleeing Apache-Yavapai from the South, and bloodthirsty Anasazi from the collapsing Chaco Canyon to the Hopi Mesas area, and eventually indirectly to the rest of the Southwest. The idea that some Sinagua became Hopi makes sense with this fact, in addition with the fact that Hopi welcomed all those fleeing persecution and suffering throughout their history. The amount of these items and their beauty in the "Priest grave", would make envy any of Sedona jewelry stores; includes long list of 25 feet strings of beads across the legs, 12 feet of beads around the priest neck, 13 shell bracelets on his arms and some five feet strings of beads around his left wrist. The combination of black-turquoise beads were tied on the priest's right side with the beautiful mosaic of the frog ears pendants and a turquoise mosaic on his chest. A lot of naked women figurines with enlarged breasts were found in the gravesite of this important man. It seems that virgins played an important role in Sinagua's afterlife passage, as well. The trade items found in the Tuzigoot excavations spoke about very extensive trade in many corners of the American Southwest, as far as the northern coast of Baja California, with their seashells and Abalone items. The parrot bones are found, imported from the Mexican jungles, and Macaw parrots were depicted on the exceptionally decorated pottery, that could not be found anywhere else, only in Tuzigoot. The pottery found was local and imported of various backgrounds, from the nearby Prescott Patayan to, as far as, Virgin Anasazi. Extraordinary pots, the beautiful Sinagua's Jeddito black on yellow were found in Tuzigoot, which set apart Sinagua as a special culture in this center of the American Southwest. Sinagua unique Native American culture was almost hidden from the public even before Tuzigoot was excavated, and went mostly unknown in the American academia. Up to this moment, the official American archeology had the problem of how to classify Sinagua; as the part of Mogollon, as Harold Colton try to or the Patayan, as McGregor attempts to or as the part of mixture of, Salado-Mimbres-Sinagua's group. Enough material evidence was not found at that time to give Sinagua the independent cultural status, yet everybody saw in plain sight, that Sinagua have their distinctive cultural traits with special attributes, which makes the Sinagua Culture apart from any others. Sinagua carried more burden because of their uniquely American cultural heavyweight since it was indigenous, and unlike any other surrounding Pre-Columbian Southwest cultures that extend ties to Mesoamerica, or to Baja California via Colorado delta, even to the Sonoran Desert. Anasazi are, on the other hand, the Aztec cult that arrived late from Mexico, and did eventually returned to the south changing the Mogollon Culture in the process of their retreat to the

Casas Grande. Navajo and Apache first came to Sedona in 1400s, as they arrived from areas of Canada or Alaska and Sinagua origin trails were nowhere to be traced to. After the last Ice Age, Clovis Culture is believed to be extinct in a sudden shift of climate change when the climate warmed up in the eastern half of the United States, and suddenly got cold again for less than a hundred years. Most of the scientists believe that in this sudden shift all the great mammals had to perish, including Mastodons, Mammoth and Sabretooth, and the Giant Bears. The archaic culture older than 7,500 years is never found in the Southwest. Today, many believe that the small groups of the Clovis Culture's last survivors crossed the Great Mississippi heading west. Could it be that at least some Sinagua are their direct descendants, nestled in central Arizona?

Montezuma Castle

The recent finds at nearby Montezuma Castle shed new light just on what happened to the late Sinagua. Sincer the Montezuma Castle is a very short distance from Tuzigoot Monument, and contemporary to it, these unfortunate events left a mark on Tuzigoot, as well. The Castle is nestled in the cliffs right on 17 freeway, exits 293 and 298 east from Sedona, and Montezuma Castle was well-known to early pioneers and is excavated before the Tuzigoot. What was puzzling, like in Tuzigoot, was the question, " What happened to Sinagua?" Even though Sinagua populated the Verde Valley, as early as, 600 A.D. The construction of Montezuma Castle did not start until 1100 A.D. and was completed around 1200 A.D. Montezuma Castle has been the driving spot for the tourists for decades, because of iconic, well-preserved dwellings, lush greenery, with its easy access from freeway 17, and stunning architecture. The Castle sits on 27-meter elevation above Beaver Creek which encompass over 4000 square feet of the dwelling spaces, built five levels high. The most recent archeological evidence from late 2016 says that Montezuma Castle did meet the final violent end, most likely by the incoming Yavapai, the entire Castle was burnt, however, the nearby Tuzigoot area was not affected. Despite the fact the Castle was very well protected by its high defense walls, the population of only a few families was not large enough to hold off, or they were surprised by the assault. It is well known for Sinagua that they will always burn their abandoned buildings and villages, but before putting them on the fire, Sinagua had a custom to seal off the major entrance from the main building with the small door and this walled off entry door is missing in this Montezuma Castle case. Despite being burnt, all Montezuma Castle seventeen rooms are in great condition for their age. The Castle was strategically positioned high above the Beaver Creek and has a year round running water, which provided necessary water irrigation for prosperous Sinagua agricultural fields and those Montezuma Castle families. Sinagua here grew corn, squash, beans, cotton, and they were involved in widespread trade, both domestic and international, just like in the case of Tuzigoot's inhabitants. Corn was their major product and it is estimated that in the Castle's good years, Sinagua produced five times more food than they would need. Sinagua did trade food for the other items primarily with the Northern Sinagua, since the soil in the north is not that fertile, and this colder climate reduces the growing season. Montezuma Castle was built with the small limestone blocks mixed with mortar and is covered with the sycamore timber, overlaid by grass, sticks, and few inches of mud. Unlike at the Anasazi sites, where timber was pine and was hauled, as far as, seventy miles away from the construction zone, Sinagua chose local wood, juniper and sycamore. Montezuma Castle could have been reached by climbing it in two ways, one is from a valley floor with ladders, and the other from a steep side of the cliffs. The junction of the wall, has a small smoke residue that filled the room, probably as an entry post. Those smaller inner rooms with a square doorway were built to conserve the heat. The heat was conserved, also, with southern exposure to the sun lights throughout the year. The Montezuma Castle building site is naturally protected by their high cliffs from the northern winds and from the cold air of Beaver Creek down below. Even in drought conditions this place looks like the Garden of Eden. The violence or disease would be the only two factors to push Sinagua out of the small paradise. No excavation has been conducted since 1930', with the exception of that small survey done in 1980, however, recent work conducted by the U.S. National Park archaeologist Matt Guebard in 2016, revealed in his new find, which supports the stories of the violent end of, at least some of the Sinagua's towns and villages. In December of 2016, Matt Guebard published his findings that all four bodies were buried in the same grave and three out of four had their skulls crushed right before the bodies were burnt. Four individuals had visible cuts on their bones, with the fractured limbs right before their death. Since Montezuma Castle supported at least 20-30 individuals at the time of their new abandonment, it is expected to conclude that some of the refugees went to Tuzigoot, or even further north with their stories. There has been a recent extensive work done by Mr.Guebard who interviewed local tribal leaders in order to find more oral narratives about those events that their ancestors may have witnessed. Several members of Yavapai-Apache clans did have some oral history in the stories their late ancestors passed down and there were descriptions of the joint effort of Apache and Yavapai in their goal to drive the Sinagua out. One Tonto Apache man did recollect the stories, when his ancestors joined Yavapai to burn Sinagua out of Montezuma Castle. Another member of Bearstrap Clan recollected the story of Sinagua villagers rushing up to the Castle and pulling up the ladders fleeing attackers. Yavapai oral history holds; the attackers set the whole Montezuma Castle on fire. This event took place around 1375-1395. It has been thought previously that Sinagua left because of disease and that this burning is just the ritual event, which was practiced before Sinagua settlements were abandoned. This is just one more important event before the Ancient Pueblo left their old settlements, sealing off their main entrance doors. This is more visible in the Chaco Canyon, but also at the Honanki's main structure. Previously all evidence of the abandonment was attributed to the accidental fire, some rituals, and unlikely to the violence, which was eliminated as the cause of these fires. In 1300, the drought did not affect Southern Sinagua but did affect their northern Anasazi neighbors to the because most of their irrigation-collection water systems that Anasazi depended on failed with the Apache and Yavapai new arrivals seeking a better life. It is very important to understand that the picture of a known ferocious Apache warrior seen in most western movies doesn't apply for this time in history, because Conquistadors have not arrived in Pueblo's Southwest yet. Once the Apache and Comanche acquired a deadly weapon called horse, which helped them to become the best cavalry that the World has ever seen, the Pueblo history did change. At this point, Apache were on foot, armed with bow and arrow, which gave Sinagua, at least, some chance. The last date of Sinagua occupation of this site falls around 1424 A.D.

Montezuma Well

Montezuma Well is a cliff dwelling Sinagua community just a short six miles drive north from Montezuma Castle. Montezuma Well is one of the most interesting geological finds in the whole American Southwest, aside being the important Sinagua agricultural Village. The Well is around 470 meters in diameter wide with large natural geological sinkhole that never dries out. There is limestone tunnel filled with the underground water which supplies Montezuma Well with its carbon dioxide-rich constant stream and since there is lack of oxygen with rich arsenic content that is found in the lake, there is almost no life that is populating Well. Exceptions are leech and moss that can thrive in this kind of under oxygenated environment. Through its inside outlet hole, the Well output a million and a half gallons of water, which gave Sinagua enough water to dugout side irrigation channels that have very nice walkway down and around the well toward Beaver Creek that never dries out. The population of Montezuma Well probably peaks around the year 1300. The first inhabitants of the Montezuma Well seem to be Hohokam, and there is one of the best-preserved Hohokam pit houses left intact and can be visited along the road leading to Well. On the bottom floor of the Hohokam pithouse there is a scale-down model, it presents how the house looked at the time it was populated. This isolated Hohokam's house does not mean that the Hohokam populated the area, because Montezuma Well way too far north from the Hohokam territory, but this can be the house of the one local Hohokam merchants, as it was the case further north in the northern Sinagua territory. The sporadic finds of the Hohokam ball courts, single houses, and the trade items prompt some previous researchers to think of many more Hohokam colonies in the north of the Sinagua territory. Today's this is viewed as a trade outpost, and the extraordinary amount of trade items are found, such as the pottery and exotic seashells, which speaks about extensive trade among the cultures of the Southwest. For nowadays existing Indian cultures in the area, the Montezuma Well represents the place where souls were born and the single connection to Sipapu underworld. For Hopi these legends of their origins tell the tales of the people originating from Sipapu underground and that this world only represents their temporary station. How Sinagua view the Well is not known, but their views should not be much different then the views of the Hopi oral traditions, that speak about the Great Water Serpent, whose spirit still dwells here in the Well. Several endemic animal species are populating the waters of Montezuma Well, and this includes the endemic Montezuma Well's leech that feeds on the endemic algaes, water scorpion species, endemic Montezuma snail and endemic shrimp-like antipodes. The very high contents of this Well's carbon dioxide is eighty times higher than in any other lake, and makes this ecosystem unique in the World. Next to the nearby rim, there is an old bank of the river a long time gone, with the two small Pueblos. Montezuma Well was the Sinagua's third settlement with seventeen rooms. This makes the location of Montezuma Well as one of the most valuable agricultural operations in ancient times.

The V-Bar-V Petroglyph site is the Sinagua's most important single recorded heritage site, the richest collection of Sinagua petroglyphs, ever found, anywhere. The V-Bar-V Heritage site is easy to get to, follow the directions from the exit 198 from freeway I-17, which is the same exit for Sedona, except you will turn to the left. V-Bar-V is very unique and since Sinagua did not leave any written records, nor a conclusive oral narrative, V-Bar-V represents Sinagua's "Hall of Records". There are no collections of Sinagua's pictorial history anywhere else, which could provide information for anthropologists and archaeologists in the years to come. Astro-astronomer Ken Zoll believes that aside from the rich and unique Sinagua's petroglyphs collection, V-Bar-V Heritage site turns out to be the largest Sinagua timekeeping sun clock or the astronomical instrument. The spirals is found on one of its panels and just like the identical spirals found in the other Sinagua panels in the Sedona sites that may in conjunction with the shadow produced by the stone slabs inserted in the crack of the rock above the spiral, produce the accurate division of year seasons as well as the time of the day, this new find was proposed by geologist Paul Lindberg, resident of Sedona. All of the V-Bar-V 13 panels put together produces collectively more than a thousand engraved images, which is called petroglyph if etched in the rock, or pictograph if painted. The carvings on the Panel must have been work by the Sinagua resident of nearby Pueblo ruins, which were strategically positioned along the Beaver Creek and the V-Bar-V petroglyph site stood as a reminder of the Sinagua story for all the travelers along the Beaver Creek trail that had been heavily visited and trafficked in the ancient past. Recent rock studies based on the opinions of the rock art scholars and Native American interpreters alike produce the newest conclusion that the V-Bar-V petroglyphs is much more recent art that includes the time frame of 1150-1400, unlike the art at Honanki, which includes pictures that are at least 10,000 years old, plus the Yavapai and Apache art past 1400, and the graphite from the pioneer period of the 19th century. The rich

V-Bar-V petroglyphs include hundreds of the animal and human

pictures, but even more important, the geometric designs that do

include the most important ones in the form of the spirals. Most of

these spiral designs were interpreted in the past as records of their

people's migrations and the sun worshiping signs. Long time ago it

was noticed that some of the round spirals were "plain", and some

had sun rays to radiate outward from them. Many of these spirals

which have the radiating sun rays are often associated with the sun

observations, but with recent finds in the Chaco Canyon and other

Many of the Anasazi sites hold the complex sun clock timekeeping,

recording, and it seems that Sinagua borrowed, or was developing

for themselves this mechanism of the season monitoring, and their

recording. The current archeological team from the Museum of the

Northern Arizona is working on the complex timekeeping sites on

the Mesas north of the Wupatki National Monument that was the

most northern edge of those Sinagua outposts bordering Anasazi territory. This complex system of the sun seasons observation is a very complex one and could have had some practical applications when it comes to the agricultural planting and harvesting seasons, and in the Sinagua case included placing the rock in the art panel, cracks that would produce the shadows on the spirals. The shadow hit the center of the spiral during the summer solstice, or at the far edge on the winter solstice. During the equinox, the shadow would cast in the middle of the spirals. This makes the V-Bar-V Heritage site not only the Sinagua's "Hall of Records", but an astronomical center for the entire culture Sinagua since it is the largest collection of petroglyphs on the single site in the whole of Arizona. On four days of the year; on spring and fall equinoxes, winter and summer solstices people gather at the V-Bar-V Heritage Site to observe this astronomical wonderland made by artistic, sun-obsessed Sinagua. This astronomical center was studied by local Astro-archeologist Kenn Zoll who proved that Sinagua observed the Sun Clock and were involved in Astro-astronomy.

Sacred Mountain

Sacred Mountain is a Butte which is visible from Montezuma Well, and is situated on the ancient trail which connects all Sinagua sites from Verde Valley to Northern Sinagua in the Flagstaff area. On the top of the butte there are the remains of the 50-60 room Pueblo with the classical built Ball Court in center, which looks like a very small depression in the field of the butte. Because of the Ball Court, and the enormous amounts of the shattered pottery pieces in the ground, Sacred Mountain must have a very significant spiritual meaning to the Southern Sinagua. Today the Sacred Mountain Pueblo is still an active archaeological site and could only be accessed with the same road continuing from the V-Bar-V Heritage Site further to the east. You can reach the white mesa with its little parking lot, by passing through the cattle gate, the trail will lead up to the top of the Sacred Mountain. Standing on the top of the Sacred Mountain, you could see Verde Valley below with its huge agricultural field which the

University of Arizona surveyors estimated to be over eighty hectar

of the endless irrigation canals, divided in primary, secondary and

tertiary branches. These canal irrigation systems were so large they

Should have easily made any Hohokam people envy. This Sacred

Mountain Pueblo is positioned in the close proximity to Red Tank

Draw, Montezuma Well, Montezuma Castle, and V-bar-V, so that

this cluster of the most Important Sinagua's sites speak about the

importance of the Palatkwapi Trail. The large amount of shattered

pottery is spread on the ground and fragments of pottery is usually

attributed to the ritual offerings of the material possessions, with

detaching themselves from their material world, and leaving this

material world behind them in favor of a spiritual one. This form

of the "purification" is commonly used by today's Pueblo Indians

of the American Southwest. One Zuni Pueblo pottery maker did

say; "From clay we came and to clay we shall return!"

Red Tank Draw

Red Tank Draw is only accessible with SUV so it is recommended to take the "Jeep Pink Tours" available at several points in Sedona. Whether you decide to take your adventures on your own from the V-Bar-V Heritage Site, turn left onto FR 689 (marked as a Beaver Creek Rd), after 1.5 miles (2.41 km) after passing the cattle guards you will reach three-way forks. Take a left fork 644H that will take you straight to the edge of Red Tank Draw. Aside from the thirteen large panels found at V-Bar-V Heritage Site, Red Tank Draw is the largest Sinagua's rock art collection in Arizona. There are sixteen locations, eight on each side of Red Tank Draw before the bridge and four, two on each side, after the bridge. Red Tank Draw center of the Sinagua ancient trade route toward Mogollon country. Rock Art petroglyphs could be; anthropomorphic (manlike), zoomorphic, (animal-like), and geometric. Red Tank Draw is the sun clock time keeping site, and is the largest found so far, aside from small panel at Honanki. Sinagua made sophisticated petroglyphs in a so-called indirect carving where two stone tools were used to chisel the stone dots. Red Tank Draw have the most beautiful zoomorphic pictures or the animal-like pictures ever found, which includes; bobcat, elk, and what appeared to be the tortoises chiseled out in more detailed way, on which the artists spend an enormous amount of time. This Sinagua time clock must have been more than the individual artist's expression, it involves the community with an important collective consciousness which binds the Sinagua religious messages. This is Sinagua's history record from the beginning of time to the mythical creatures portrayed in Sinagua petroglyphs which played the major role in the Sinagua history. Red Tank Draw is believed to be just a station alongside the famous Palatkwapi Trail in Northeast Arizona, crossing over the Mogollon Rim, all the way to Verde Valley that ends in minefields of what is today, ghost town Jerome. Red Tank Draw is supposed to remind the travelers of the story of Sinagua on their way to the rich mineral mines in Jerome's area. The Red Tank

Draw's close proximity to Montezuma Well adds to the importance of each site, since Montezuma Well represents to Hopi, Zuni, and Yavapai-Apache tribes the point of their origin, or Sipapu in Hopi language. The most important message that is left for these cultures throughout their historical existence is to commemorate their story with a significant amount of written records, and if the culture had no written language, then only the visual images of that culture can speak about the origin or point of destruction important for the one particular culture. Montezuma Well could be representing the portal toward another inter-dimension, an underground world of emerging souls which is in Hopi tradition the portal where human souls came from in the migration journey through the Hopi first Three Worlds. Yavapai hold very similar views of their underworld, therefore, the proximity of the Palatkwapi trail and Montezuma Well contribute to a significance of Red Tank Draw. Both Honanki and Palatki speak about the destruction of Sinagua in the famous Hopi Legend of the Lost City of Palatkwapi.

Honanki

To reach Honanki ruins from intersection known as the Y, which is considered as the unofficial center of Sedona, follow Highway 89A toward Cottonwood, turn right onto Dry Creek Rd, and follow Dry Creek road until you reach the T intersection with Boynton Canyon Pass. Turn left to Boynton Canyon Pass Rd., then keep right which will become 125C Rd. for a brief moment, and then merge in 525A to the right. Turn left, onto the N Loy Butte Rd. You will reach the Honanki, which is today, the National Historic Landmark. All the walkways are clearly marked and explained so that the excavations are not disturbed. Native Americans have an emotional or spiritual connection to them. It gives the Native community some sense of their tribe passage of time, lineage to divine, and their origins, as it holds the proof of origin and ownership of land. Hegelian academia advocates would be proud of a job well done. Most researchers do believe today that Sinagua moved to the Hopi Mesas to the north in

1400, so the future DNA research may prove the genetic lineage to Hopi. The word Honanki means, The Bear House in Hopi, but other than name there is no other oral connection to Hopi tribe. The name simply means that Hopi were aware of these ancient ruins, however, no evidence exists that there is any story connection to the Sinagua living there, or what has happened to all them. The first and the last time Honanki was fully excavated was during the first 1895-1911 excavation of the Smithsonian Institute led by Jesse Walter Fawkes as a part of the Hopi migration study. Jesse Walter Fewkes noted in his works that the Sedona red rocks are carved in such a shape that they resembled the ancient Greek temples or cathedrals, and sooner or later this discovery would become the spot of the sightseer. This prophetic sentence was made in May of 1895, and nobody has ever excavated Honanki since, except recently in 1999, as a part of this new research called, the Verde Valley Archeology Association, that is still going on. During this excavation, a groundbreaking find did come to light of the day, where during his restroom time stop one of the researchers found the Clovis Culture arrow point. This would push the presence of the Paleo Indians, that continuously occupied the site for more than 10,000 years. This natural cliff caved shelter has provided great hideout even before the basket weaving periods. The Pueblo Culture is classified and organized in the four periods, after the Paleo and Archaic periods. The first of these periods has been described as the Basket making period and is followed by the pottery making period. Next, follows the drywall or the brick and mortar period with the building culmination of the Great Kivas in the Chaco Canyon, Mesa Verde and Aztec Ruin, the great cities of Anasazi, all in New Mexico. The Southern Sinagua culmination of the building organized town is represented in the towns of Honanki, Palatki, Montezuma Castle, and the largest of all of them, Tuzigoot National Monument in Clarkdale. Unlike the most famous culture, the Chaco Canyon which was abandoned during the great drought period of 1350s, where we found evidence of warfare and violence followed by the exodus to the Mesa Verde, Cortez, and Aztec Ruin sites, there is no evidence of any violence in Honanki. The visible, and only known evidence of fire is to the east part of the ruins that were rebuilt sometimes in the last phase of building Honanki. Most of the Archeologists agree there are at least three phases of building the Honanki and which is dated between 1130-1280, and one of the three beams has examined for the tri-ring dating confirmed the year 1271. By year 1400 the Honanki site was abandoned as the Sinagua Village and has been sporadically populated by the arriving Apache and the Yavapai bands, according to the visible pictographs on site. Yavapai-Apache finally left the area in 1875, when displaced to the San Carlos Reservation. The archaeological excavation is ongoing at a very slow pace due to the lack of financing and permits that do depend on tribal approval. The Honanki Village falls in the Pecos III classification building site and this includes a large village rather than a more organized town. The Village does not have the rounded Kivas as their primary religious/gathering site, but no other Sinagua town ever had. This is just one of many unique features, which does distinguish Sinagua from the Meso-American Cult, which occupied and influenced the Chaco Canyon Anasazi culture. Sinagua villages and towns had special rooms, such as several rooms in the center of Tuzigoot National Monument and they served as the ceremonial or religious rooms, were rectangular and not center located. All of the building materials for the housing, clay pottery and designs lacking round Kiva, and very position of residential vs. community rooms pointing to a unique culture apart from Anasazi. Researchers hold that there is an ethnic link to Anasazi but not to the modern Pueblo tribes. The only exception is Peter Pilles and his early controversial idea that the Yavapai are right claiming that there were in the area forever, because they intermarry Sinagua. Yavapai coexisted with Sinagua for 100-150 years before Sinagua disappeared. The recent excavation at Honanki site revealed the extraordinary amount of the new archeological evidence, with the large number of artifacts that doubled the collection excavated at Montezuma Castle that proves same and consistent cultural tie between the Sinagua towns around the Verde Valley. The rich finds in weaving and textile technologies were superb to all other weaving techniques at that time throughout the American Southwest, and it seems the technique is passed down to the modern Western Pueblo. The pottery technique was superb to Prescott gray on black pottery however, it is not as good quality as ones found in the Anasazi north. The Pottery found does have those classical red on yellow color, and their very distinctive art patterns. Other artifacts found at Honanki were the ritual and the ceremonial Pachos prayer sticks, which are the religious sticks wrapped up in a yucca fibers or cotton yarns that are used in prayers, and are found among the nowadays Hopi tribe. It does look that, aside from those weaving-dyeing style in their clothing, the Sinagua passed to Hopi religious objects as well. In the center of Honanki complex, there is a beautiful and large red-brown image of the Grizzly Bear, possibly prompted Hopi to name the village,"The Bear House". Large round Grizzly bear petroglyph stands in the center of the largest dwelling at Honanki. The most prominent petroglyph is the "Flute player", which portrays the "Puchteca", a common trader flute player from Mesoamerica who would always play his flute, announcing arrival in the town. Another such character that is singled out by the most visitors' is "the Basketball player", and it seems that he slams his ball into the basket, according to the rock art experts, he is the "Sun watcher" with his special tool, and what looks like the "basketball" could be representation of the Sun. The older petroglyphs found are much more geometric-gloomy white, dating from the older archaic periods, according to Peter Pilles. Those petroglyphs of the archaic periods found are estimated to be over five thousand years old and should never depict human-like or animal-like figures. The next are the Yavapai-Apache petroglyphs section that are present in the post Honanki period, as well as, the most recent Pioneer's arts graphites. The archeological leftover graphites suggest that Honanki was used as the temporary shelter by many groups after Sinagua left the site. The people who prefer the Hopi connection, therefore, the full Hopi continuity of the Sinagua history, point out, to rich Hopi legend of the origin of the Hopi Water Clan, that came from the Honanki and Palatki sites after the "Great Flood", and the great earthquake, that preceded the flood event. Honanki is a rich place in the Paleoindian, Archaic, Sinagua, and Apache-Yavapai petroglyphs, however, Hopi design style petroglyphs are still missing? The fact tells us that long after the last surviving Sinagua had left for the North, whether they joined Hopi at the Hopi mesas, as all the other refugees did, fleeing Spanish Inquisition, and Kit Carson raids which have followed, or they perished in increased Apache-Yavapai raids in following years 1300-1400, one fact is certain, neither Hopi nor Sinagua ever came back to Honanki, again. Hopi and Zuni today, come back to Sedona and their holy place includes Honanki, where the Hopi Water Clan members can identify the insignia petroglyph as the clan's insignia. This oral history does not hold enough proof, in order to conclude a direct lineage from Sinagua to Hopi and Zuni, however, this is both plausible and probable, that the last surviving Sinagua joined Hopi, especially the Water Clan. The Hopi Water Clan today focuses on everything that comes from Honanki, because they have a rich oral history of Honanki origins, and is the first Clan populated both the Honanki and Palatki sites. According to the Hopi's oral history, the Water Clan is the first Clan to lead all the others to their migrations from Sedona in the south to the north, and after "the fall" of Great Red City of Palatkwapi, the last Sinagua refugees join Hopi at what is nowadays the Hopi Mesas. Hopi claims that the spiral circles left on the thousands of petroglyphs, which is the evidence of the divine order of their clan migrations, and all the journeys and migrations in this world are orderly guided. Hopi do recognize messages from the petroglyphs, and even the signs of their Water Clan. During recent excavations at Honanki, Hopi identified the prayer sticks, called the Pachos worn by the religious leader of the Clan.

Palatki

Palatki is the most mysterious Sinagua site. Palatki translates as the Red House and is according to author Mark Pinkham, short version of name Palatkwapi, which is the most mythological sacred city for Hopi, and is the place of emerging of their souls, coming of Sipapu, underground world. Mesoamericans also believe in this version of the origins of the people as the American Indians of the Southwest. Another importance of Palatki is nearby red cliff rock petroglyphs and pictographs from only two periods; from Archaic times that are 5000 to 6000 years old and the Sinagua time period that is between 600-1425 A.D. The Yavapai-Apache graphites and recent Pioneer graphites are missing unlike in the case of Honanki. That Pioneers and Yavapai-Apache absence of their Palatki habitation is observed by Jesse Walter Fewkes, in May 1895, as Jesse W. Fewkes, who is the first archaeologist that had found Palatki just by accident as he had already excavated Honanki, in almost pristine condition before the treasure hunters. Palatki amounts for more than a one thousand petroglyphs present which predates the Palatki Ruins, and testifies the importance of the Palatki site. The only question remaining is, why Honanki has been visited by Apache-Yavapai in the past, and Hopi in present and why Palatki was in its intact condition upon a Jesse W. Fewkes arrival in 1895? Was Palatki really an unknown place or was it, perhaps, "do not go to place?" We might find this answer in one of the most celebrated Hopi legends about the linear passages of time in the Hopi last Four Worlds. The Hopi saga gives special importance to the legend of the lost city of Palatkwapi and their Water Clan exodus to the north. Hopi speak the Uto-Aztecan language which points to the arrival sometimes two thousand years ago from the Mesoamerican South. The First Hopi's creation story narrative, that was collected by Harold Courlander, begins with the creation of the "First World", with its first opening words; "In the beginning, there was only the Endless Space, there was no light, no wind, no shadows. Tawe, the Sun Spirit was the only One in all the existence, with some lesser Gods. Tawe was disappointed because what Tawe did help create was more imperfect. Tawa said, "What I have created was imperfect and all the creatures do not understand the meaning of life?" Tawe sent his messenger, a woman called the Spider Grandmother to show Tawe's creatures their only way to the underworld, after all, the creatures did emerge in the Second World and the creatures were different in the Second World. The animals did resemble animals that we see today; dogs, coyotes, and bears alike. The emerged creatures did not have a slight understanding of one another, and they fought and even ate each other. While these creatures travel guided by the messenger women Tawa created the 'Third World". The new creatures lost all their fur, claws, tails, so they do look quite different. The messenger of God appeared now as the Spider Grandmother has spoken to creatures; "You are now, the people!" The Spider Grandmother reminded the people; Tawa created you out of the Endless Space and Tawa gave you this place so you people of this World could and should live in harmony, and forget all evil. So Hopi started their sinless life in the Third World. This Hopi legend of their lost Red City Palatkwapi, makes Palatki village the synonym for the Red House and reminds listeners to the common biblical saga of their twin cities of Sodom and Gomorrah, and if both Honanki and Palatki are, in fact, the possible location of mysterious lost city located southwest of the present Hopi Land, the story of Mankind Fall became more similar. The Hopi legend of the World origins continues with a new formed people, the band calling itself, the Patki Woema. Patki band moved from the south in their boat, and escaped the endless wickedness floating on the water and their name itself means, the "dwelling on the water". This name has been passed down to the Water Clan of Hopi and for origin of Hopi Water Clan, legend says that they came from Palatkwapi after the second disaster, and arrived at the Hopi Mesa. This is in support of all those anthropologists and historians who believe that the Hopi Water Clan originated from Sedona Sinagua and merged with many other Hopi Clans. After their arrival at the place called Palatkwapi,

Hopi Water Clan formed their first village and with the arrival of Cloud, Frog, Tobacco, Rabbit, Eagle, Hawk, Sun, Sand, and Brush clans the great City of Palatkwapi. Many Clan members recall the Hopi legend of the Great Red City Palatkwapi's fall, which speaks about the significance and the importance of Sedona, Verde Valley in general for all these great migrations, and congregation of their people at one site. Hopi Water Clan was first to arrive and lead the people in the ancient past to this day, and the Water Clan members today visit Sedona to pay respect to the ancestors. This is the point where Hopi narrative ends, where the scientists are looking for the missing link between Sinagua and the modern Hopi tribe. The Hopi saga continues that their life was good and that most people become forgetful about their old ways and their obligations. The people did continue the migrations to the place called Flower Mound, however, most people turned to be evil to wickedness and corruption. Instead of coming to the place of worship, which is their great Kiva, and to discuss the meaning of life, the people have turned the great Kiva into a place for gamble and people stop making the Pachos or their prayer sticks, the young people forgot to take care of their elders. Even more, the young began to harass the weak and old, neglecting the work in the fields, the married women have been lying with the men who were not their husbands. The cloud of darkness gleaned in its mist over the Great Red City Palatkwapi. It is held by the official American Anthropology that the oldest ancient Puebloan Kachina Cult originated sometimes between 1300-1400 and this corresponds with the change in religious beliefs, due to a major traumatic event that occurred in the American Southwest. In the core origins of this legend, of the rise and the destruction of Palatkwapi, the great Kiva was viewed as the place of worship, and the prayer sticks known as Pachos, are found to this day, however, the Hopi legend now for the first time evolves into the appearance of the Kachina Cult. Legend continues with the leaders of Hopi people led by Chief Kikmongwi had chosen the young boy and dressed him in costume of the Tsavo Monster sent him to hunt for the deer as the sacrificial offering.

The Tsaveyo Monster was to be dressed in the buckskin cape, with a quiver full of arrows, carried a bow and large ax in his hands. The young Boy that dressed as Tsavo Monster was supposed to carry the message to all the wicked and wearing several Kachina style masks in the layers, much like the Russian Babushka Dolls. Instructed by legendary Water Clan chief Kikmongwi the young man dressed as Tsaveyo gave the sermon to Hopi, but was ignored and many went back to Kiva, only to gamble. Palatkwapi now returned to the final fall of the Third World. After his failed sermon Kikmongwi and his nephew tried to send a message to the people of Red Palatkwapi for the second time. Chief Kikmongwi instructs his nephew to hunt for the deer in the mountain and after the ritual sacrifice, take the horn of the deer as the personal talisman. In the classic tale of religious animism, Chief Kikmongwi's nephew speaks to the deer, explains why deer needed to die. The deer agreed to die holding the Pachos, prayer sticks that can assure the deer passage to the afterlife. Young man took the deer's horn and placed it on its head and this talisman was supposed to give the transfer of the animal spirit to the young man and empower the message to the fallen people of the Red City Palatkwapi. Armed with the four kachina masks which were placed over one another and with the necklace made of the human bones, the young man went to the Palatkwapi one more time and delivered the message on the top of the Kiva. Chief Kikmongwi's nephew has warned the people a few more times the magic fire will run over the villages witnessed by the Palatkwapi residents. Anger broke up and so the young man was taken from the Kiva's roof and after the long interrogation, he was publicly lynched. What prompted this lynch, was the fear of those Kachina masks that Kikmongwi's nephew was wearing? The first mask, which was taken from the young man was Kiwa mask, that is the mask of Kachina dancers and second was the Owhalani mask, the mask is used today in the Soyal dance and the third was the Talavai mask, used today by the Dawn Kachinas, and last was the Masauwu mask, which was the spirit of the death mask that made Palatkwapi sinners particularly disturbed. The young man chewed the special medicine which made his breath fire and with a very special breath of Masauwu, the spirit of the death. The people in Palatkwapi rejected all his warnings and killed their messenger. The Fourth World saga, continues with the last wish of the lynched messenger in which the people of Palatkwapi have to leave the deer horn on the top of his head and with one of his hands unburied. On the fourth morning, the earthquake struck Palatkwapi and its walls collapsed. The sky turned dark gray and blurry, and the Sun turned shiny red and the great flood followed the earthquake, and most of the people died. The Great Palatkwapi was the great Red City of the Fourth World, since it was completely in ruins, people had to start living their lives again as they did in the Third World (Courlander, 1971). Some Clans went west, never to be heard from again, and all those who went south were killed on the way. The Legend says that only one clan went north, and survived on the Palatkwapi trail.

Shaman's Cave

Shaman's Cave is one of the last Sedona vortexes to be discovered by the modern spiritual seekers, however, and it was the important religious place for nearby Palatki and Honanki Sinagua residents. Shaman's Cave has been used for centuries in the religious Sinagua ceremonies and it is marked with petroglyphs that faded away with time, including the 13-foot-long Snake petroglyph painted into the Cave's floor which is hard to see due to the tooth of time. Shaman's Cave is located in very close proximity to Palatki and using google maps, do not turn to the 525C like the directions instruct you and do not follow the GPS; instead, follow 525C until you see road mark split to 9530 to your right. Follow road 525C for the half-mile with the high clearance vehicle which is a must for the last half mile or so. The hike is very light and moderately steep. The Shaman's Cave vortex location is on top of the actual giant egg-shaped cave, and it has been known to the local spiritual seekers as the Shaman's Cave

Dome vortex. The local spiritual seekers claim that the Cave is one of the most powerful vortexes, if not the most powerful portal to the other dimensions, yet the least traveled one. The dome is formed by the million years of Mother Nature's carving it with its winds and rain that has resulted in the water sculpted egg shape cave made of quartz sandstone. The combination of quartz eggshell, ferrous rich soil, with the underground water flow, made the whole Sedona one giant geological wonder and made its spiritual resonance possible. The San Francisco Peaks are the three-headed mountain peaks and are richest water reservoir in the entire Arizona, converging all of the underground rivers in this natural aqueduct. Partially is visible as the creeks and streams that contribute to Verde Valley River, and partially is invisible. Underground rivers made a hidden catacombs, and caverns under Sedona that resulted in forming all the sinkholes around the town. This underground invisible world must have been the source of the legend of the Ancient Red City Palatkwapi and its Sipapu, the underground world which is the origin of the souls. This vast rich water outflow exit near Page Springs not far from the new Sinagua Tuzigoot City, is a drinkable one. Another giant opening of this water supply is Montezuma Well which is sacred for Yavapai, Apache, Hopi and Zuni. Shaman's Cave sits on the water aqueduct, and there are several sinkholes around the area. Shaman's Cave is sealed off by a steep cliff below its entrance by the drywall that has only a small waist height entrance to the Cave. The Cave surface is flat and rounded with one circular window from which magnificent view is open toward southwest, giving the viewer 180-degree visual joy of the Valley below. Night covered with the full Moon light that peers in the Cave could be even more spectacular. The wall around the Cave has disappearing petroglyphs, and its flat floor has holes most likely used for preparing the medicine for the Sinagua ritual ceremonies. The natural encroachment of the egg-shaped Shaman's Cave and its ceiling makes the perfect spot for solitary meditation.

Fay Canyon

Fay Canyon is less traveled and less known vortex east of Palatki, it is accessible from West Sedona driving on 179A westbound, exit on Dry Creek Rd. to the right, and continue on Dry Creek Rd, until you reach the T intersection. Turn left on Boynton Canyon Rd, you will face another T intersection. Turn to left on the Boynton Pass road, in 0.5 miles you will reach the Fay Canyon parking lot to your left. The area around parking is clearly marked, however, you will have to cross the Boynton Pass Road on foot, heading north to trail. Once you start heading up in between the two hills which formed the Fay canyon, you will notice the beautiful formation named, Wine Glass to your right side at the very beginning of the hill. Fay Canyon trail is moderate, and some 2.2 miles round trip its length total, however, the Fay Canyon Arch intersection is located some 0.5 miles into the trail itself. The GPS coordinates for the Fay Canyon Trail are N34 54.105 W111 51.469. The right turn toward the Arch is not marked anymore, so you have to look to the human foot-shaped rock to the east as a marker. Just recently, hikers made the white circle in small rock obstructing the trail, about half-way into the Fay Canyon trail, turn to the right of the marked rock up to the hill. The Fay Canyon Arch is located to the immediate left of a giant rock in the shape of a human foot that is positioned up from the ground. This foot-like rock formation can be viewed from the other side of the hill, as well as, from the Boynton Canyon's Kachina Woman formation, and the Boynton Canyon Vista as well. As you hike this very steep trail up the hill, you will see the Fay Canyon Arch more clearly against its background rock. The Fay Canyon vortex is located right under the giant arch with its natural cut rock in the shape of a giant door. The GPS coordinates for the Fay Canyon Arch (vortex) are N34 54.582 W111 51.674. This cut made the door that is believed to be the time travel portal, according to the New Age followers, and I could not find the one Native American story that could be related to the Fay Canyon Arch. West of the Arch is just another interesting formation called the Wine Glass Rock. The Fay Canyon trail can be hiked all

to its end, where you could reach another interesting rock formation

in the shape of an angry man face and if you can climb up behind it,

there is the Sinagua Ruins outpost, in the shape of the small cottage.

This area is called Box Canyon and does extend a far away beyond

the trail. The arch area has a small observation post under the Arch,

which is made of the drywall stones and forms a small room ten by

ten under the Arch that forms a natural ceiling above this structure.

The other observation Sinagua dwelling is located at the far end of

the Fay Canyon trail, over the Angry Man's rock formation. From

this observation post, there are open unobstructed views of the Fay

Canyon trail to the south and Box Canyon to the north.

Boynton Canyon Vortex

Boynton Canyon Vortex is well documented Sinagua's sacred site, still visited by the local tribes. Boynton Canyon is home to one of the most interesting rock formations rising above vortex site that is in the form of beautiful women known to the Native Americans as the Kachina Woman Rock. The Kachina Women Rock represents Mother Earth's deity and is connected with its little rock formation which faces the south with its rock in the form of a Saddle, which represents an umbilical cord connecting Mother Earth, represented as the Kachina Woman Rock, with its child, the Little Rock Knoll. The Kachina Woman Rock with its Little Rock Knoll is the Native American version of Madonna and Child, and is built and carved in the sandstone by Mother Earth, with the winds, land, air, and rain. The symbolism seen here is more than obvious as you approach the Kachina Women Rock, even before you feel the vortex. The Major four sacred elements that are present here are; air, rainwater, wind and the sandstone dust. The Native Americans have been coming to this place for centuries and the legend said that the Kachina Woman Rock cures the infertile women. The vortex energy is the strongest between the Little Rock Knoll formation and the Kachina Women's rock. The Little Rock Knoll is a favorite spot for the tourists taking photos, since it offers 360 degrees of unobstructed views of Verde Valley, Cathedral Rock and Bell Rock, that are visible to the south. In the famous Hopi legend of the lost Palatkwapi after mankind did fall and the great red city Palatkwapi was destroyed, man fell back in the Third World and all the survivors were forced to march to the North. Those survivors were left only with the Kachina Women that was sent by Tawe, to look after them. In this story of how Kachina Women was created by Tawe the legend continues; if mankind does not go in the right direction in the Fourth World, eventually into the Fifth World, the Kachina Woman formation will crumble down and humanity will be lost forever. Short Vista Trail ends on the Saddle in-between the Kachina Woman Rock and Little Rock, which is the exact Vortex epicenter and you could find many of New Age rocks stacked on the top of each other. The Boynton Canyon and Airport Vortex are the most visited vortexes by many tourists and the New Age people alike, for its easy accessibility. From the very start of intersection 89A/179, take 89A west for 3.2 miles, turn right on the Dry Creek Road for 2.9 miles, then turn left on 152 C, and follow the Boynton Canyon sign for about 1.8 miles, the parking a lot will be on your right. From the Boynton parking lot, follow the Boynton Canyon Trail on foot to the first intersection with the Deadman Pass and turn to the left, continue until you reach T intersection with the Vista Trail. Turn right on the Vista Trail, and climb up to the Little Rock formation up above. From here, you will see Kachina Woman Rock towering above you and its little rock knoll. The last 400 feet are found to be the hardest ones, since the trail at this point is very steep. The Boynton Canyon vortex is called a combination vortex, and is a mix of the feminine and masculine energy or the inflow-outflow vortex.

Arizona Creation

Continue further on the Boynton Canyon Trail and turn to the Vista Trail leading to the Kachina Woman Rock, within 2 miles you will reach the lost Sinagua Ruins, which was in their ancient times more revered than Kachina Woman Rock today. Yavapai Nation tradition holds that there were three sacred places reserved for their creation story located in Sedona. Yavapai claim, that the trio of Montezuma Well, Mingus Mountain and Boynton Canyon is not only the center of the creation story of their people located here in Sedona but the Arizona creation. The Yavapai creation story starts at Montezuma Well like many other tribes describe the Sipapu or the underworld where the people lived, and at that time when Montezuma Well is dry. Because of the fall of man, the great flood came, water-filled Montezuma Well. There are only two remaining survivors left, the young girl and woodpecker. The young girl and woodpecker were put in a carved log by the girl's grandfather. The grandfather told his granddaughter that they are not to leave the log. The young girl and woodpecker took a long journey in log, which served as canoe for forty days and forty nights. After forty days and forty nights the water receded, the girl and the woodpecker found themselves on the highest grounds around. The girl with her white stone talisman was known from there on, as the "Old Lady with the Pearl". This white Pearl that the young girl has taken is the protection stone from the underworld. When the flood ended, the young girl did land on the highest dryland peak in Sedona, today this is the Capital Butte of the Thunder Mountain. Later the girl gave birth to the First Lady in Boynton Canyon and from this point on, the Boynton Canyon Cave became a sacred site for the Yavapai-Apache. The Boynton Canyon Cave is not so far from the Vista Trail, where the Kachina Woman Rock formation is located, and curiously even more coincidental it is not far from Palatki Ruins, where the destruction of Palatkwapi occurred, during the Great Flood in Hopi Legend of creation of the Fourth World. The divine woman in the Yavapai Legend has been freed from their log by woodpecker at the highest peak in Sedona. The young girl held a shiny white pearl, which her grandfather gave her for protection and then took the trail toward Mingus Mountain. There on at the highest peak of Mingus Mountain, she got pregnant with the Sun. On her return to Boynton Canyon, she took a bath in an enchanted pool where she discovered that she was pregnant. She gave birth to a daughter or First Lady, mother protector of Yavapai People. The Holy Virgin landed at the highest point in Sedona, that is actually the Peak of Thunder Mountain, also called Capital Butte. Arizunna is the name which means, the Sun beloved maiden, and from where the name for Arizona came from. Arizunna landed on that highest peak on Sedona's Capital Butte of Thunder Mountain. Thunder Mountain is named by major thunderstorms which fire the thunderbolts hitting from above the Capital Butte Peak. Arizunna landing at the highest peak of Sedona's Capital Butte of Thunder Mountain is the Natives creation story of Arizona.

Red Rock Crossing

The most inspiring symbol of Sedona and, perhaps, one of the most recognizable images of the American Southwest is the iconic image of Cathedral Rock that could be taken from the Red Rock Crossing State Park. These images are the most inspiring even for the people who never heard of Sedona and the images are, as recognizable as, the Monument Valley, the Devil Tower and the Black Hills photos. Hollywood movies portray conquest of the Wild West with them, such as "Midnight Run" with Robert De Niro, "Drum Beat" with Alan Ladd or "Broken Arrow" with Jimmy Stewart, just to name a few. Red Rock Crossing is part of the Cathedral Rock complex, and also part of the major Cathedral Rock Vortex. Most psychics point to the Cathedral Rock as the location of two vortexes, one is on top of the iconic Cathedral Rock between the two rock spikes, and the one down below Cathedral Rock, the Red Rock Crossing Vortex. The location of the Red Rock Crossing Vortex is right in the middle of its Oak Creek, and where the three large rocks stick

out of the Oak Creek, for the most part of the year, if there are no

floods, its epicenter is on the large rock in the middle which is dry.

Red Rock Crossing has been identified as the "inflow", "feminine"

vortex, and is used for work with inner disturbances of one's soul

considering the events that hurt an individual in the past and needs

to be resolved. With the help of the Oak Creek water flow, the spot

is perfect for cleansing of negative emotions stuck with that person.

Red Rock Crossing could be approached from the Crescent Moon

State Park and from the end of the Verde Valley School Road, north

from the Village of Oak Creek. Driving from Sedona Uptown, the

unofficial center is "Y", which is the intersection of Highways 179

and 89A, continue on 179A to West Sedona for 4.3 miles. Turn left

to the Upper Red Rock Loop road passing the Sedona High School.

After about 1.8 miles, turn to the Chavez Ranch Road, and after a

mile, enter Crescent Moon State Park. Drive, as far as you can and

continue on foot until you reach Oak Creek beach. This beach is called, "The Buddha Beach" and is all surrounded by hundreds of perfectly stack river rocks that are mimicking Chakras in the human body. When you feel that warm sensation, which only the feminine inner energy can provide, you will know that you arrived. The right brain lobe is responsible for all the creativity in the arts, humanities, language and the other profound emotions that are referred to as the "feminine" and are guided by estrogens in the human body. Every woman's and man's estrogens should spark up to the point that you will feel protected by Mother Nature; and you should feel the strong need to give and protect the others. Walking alongside Oak Creek's bedrock where giant Cathedral Rock comes closest to the water, the vortex sensation that you will feel is very strong. The last and the least traveled way to approach the Red Rock Crossing Vortex is to drive from highway 179A to Back-O-Beyond Road, some half mile from Cathedral Rock.

Cathedral Rock

Cathedral Rock is the vortex with another creation story that secret Sedona holds. This is the creation story of the relationship between the first man and the first woman. In Yavapai creation story, after the long and harsh winter, sole survivors found their refuge under Cathedral Rock, it was only one man and one woman. The couple was in a relationship that lasted through the Ice Age winter and is shaped enough to last forever. On the outside, the couple seems to have the appearance of unity and nothing should break up a strong relationship. On the inside, there was a struggle within themselves and within each other. The man has begun to accuse his women of being guilty of disastrous harsh conditions that they went through the winter, and of being different since they first met, being not as beautiful as when they first met. On the other hand, the women had similar thoughts about her man, and she was blaming him for this horrible winter that they went through. Man is blamed for being a poor hunter, spending no time with her, not being handsome. The couple struggled a lot so that they produced the enormous level of the negative energy and the dark cloud surrounded Cathedral Rock. The spirits sent by the Creator were disturbed around, so the spirits decided that they should do something. The spirits appointed their messenger, the Great Water Serpent which emerged from the Oak Creek and warned the couple for their obvious misbehavior. Then, Great Serpent rose up from the water and had spoken to the couple that they end abuse of the energy given to them by the Creator and to use this energy as they were supposed to, be more positive. The Great Serpent showed the couple how their spirits are built in the Cathedral Rock, with their bodies erect, so they stand up straight back-to-back facing the opposite direction. This way the couple is punished, by being close but not be able to see each other forever, however, they supported each other back-to-back for eternity, they looked toward their half of the world. The couple bodies turned to hard cold stone, their spirits were locked forever, looking to their world they had left, which is represented with the two joint stone towers. The Great Serpent told the couple that this way they would have their own way, and their own half of the World, but have they wish to see and embrace the opposite side of the World, they would have to see only that half, not with their own eyes, but through the partner's one. In this way, they were to work, and to communicate together if they wish to see. On the other hand, if they stay selfish, and stand their ground, they will stay blind to the other side forever. Take 89A to the south from the "Y", heading toward the Oak Creek Village. Turn right onto the Back-o-Beyond Road, half a mile to the parking area at the very bottom of Cathedral Rock on your left side, and then hike up the trail, up to the spires. The hike is only 0.7 mile one way, however the elevation change is 600 feet and this is very intense. Once you reach the two middle spires, you will notice the big granite gray rock below the spires. This small rock is called the Grandmother Rock by locals, and is the epicenter of the Cathedral Rock Vortex.

Bell Rock Vortex

Driving south toward the Oak Creek Village from the "Y", for 6.4 miles, you will reach the Bell Rock Parking lot trail on the left side, right before the Bell Rock Blvd. Turn left and watch for incoming traffic from the Oak Creek Village. From the parking lot, you will take the trail for several hundred feet where the trail will split at the Courthouse Butte Loop, which is circular five miles trail that leads to Courthouse Butte, Spaceship Rock, and Baby Bell, smaller and easier to access vortex, which is an offshoot of the Big Bell Rock. The straight arrow at the split sign will take you straight to the Big Bell Rock that is the hardest vortex to climb. Easy way to approach the Bell Rock Vortex is from the Courthouse Butte parking lot, and the Bell vortex epicenter is located on the south side of Bell Rock. The first approach, is from the southern side, recommended only for serious climbers because it is very steep. It can be approached from the Bell Rock parking lot, and from the Oak Creek Village.

For the average hiker, like me, it is easier to take the northern hike, and follow steel baskets filled with the red rocks which will lead to the end of the trail on the `` second level". The Bell Rock formation is built on levels, and the vortex energy can be felt on the first level. It is not necessary to climb all the way to the top since the vortex is located on the second level, on the southern side. Once you reach the end of the trail on the Rock's second level from northern side, It is quite a challenge to make the whole loop around the steep Bell Rock circling the western bound of it, finally reaching its southern side. That way is safer and once you reach its southern side, from where you can see Oak Creek Village, the vortex epicenter is right below the highest peak of Bell Rock's southern side. Many of the vortex twisted Juniper Trees are growing around this area, which are grown with the twisted trunk, swirled by geomagnetic vortex energy emitting from Mother Earth. The Bell Rock Vortex is the so-called balanced vortex of masculine/feminine energies. This Vortex energizes the spirit in a motivational and competitive way.

Baby Bell

People who find the climb to the top of Bell Rock a challenge could always pay a visit to smaller, bell-shaped rock, to the north of Bell Rock, called Baby Bell, which is home to a smaller vortex located in the center of the Plateau, twenty yards south of Baby Bell. Baby Bell is an easy hike which starts from the left side of the parking lot, and approaches the rock from its north side, and if you do climb to the top of Baby Bell, and you can observe those sweeping views of Sedona, and its Valley with Courthouse Butte, Rabbit Ears, and Bell Rock itself. Should you take a hike south of the Baby Bell Loop, and want to reach the Baby Bell Vortex south Plateau, then start the loop walk from the south. You will reach the Baby Bell plateau in several hundred feet, and even walking from the trail you will feel the vortex energy as you approach Baby Bell and the vortex center in the middle of Plateau with its vortex energy gradually increasing. Baby Bell is, also, a mix vortex with masculine/feminine energy.

Chapel of the Holy Cross

One of Sedona's most visited and photographed landmarks surely is the Chapel of the Holy Cross. The Chapel was carved in the rock by Marguerite Brunswig Staude, a Hungarian born sculptress in 1955. Marguerite said that she had the vision of this chapel visiting New York City, and observing the Empire State Building. She said that the idea came into her mind that the Empire State Building can be an image of the great church. From that very moment, Marguerite has begun to wander around the world looking for the most perfect location for her chapel. Marguerite's early sketch caught the eye of Lloyd Wright, the son of famous American sculptor, Frank Lloyd Wright. The initial design did not get approved by the Los Angeles archdiocese, to which Marguerite belongs to. The Archdiocese was not happy about this radical architectural design, therefore, the new Chapel had to find its new home in Budapest Hungary, where nuns were excited about the whole new design coming from America.

The start of the Second World War has disrupted this attempt, and Marguerite realized that her dream's vision should be materialized only sometime in the future. Marguerite parents died in 1940, and Marguerite's mother's last wish was that Marguerite does leave her last spiritual trust on earth. Marguerite envisioned her new church reshaped after she saw the church in France designed by the French painter Georges Rouault, and after securing all permissions with the help of Arizona Senator Barry Goldwater, construction began in the spring of 1955. Marguerite on that occasion said; "Our monument would become the chapel dedicated to finding God through the art"! Marguerite did just that, without knowing that the grounds beneath the Chapel was sacred to the Indians and is the location of vortex, just beneath the arch, encrusting the Chapel in the rock. Marguerite knew there were more, much more, which Marguerite did not want to talk about. Marguerite commissioned the large steel crucifix that used to hang above the stained glass windows from 1956 to 1977. All these years there were regular masses celebrated in the Chapel, with lectures, and retreats. Later on, there were many weddings and various other meetings at the chapel conducted, where people used to discuss the sculpture of Christ made of steel and cast in the shape of a surrealistic body that reminded people of Salvador Dali's work. The Iron crucifix was so controversial, so locals gave him a famous nickname, the Christ of Atomic Age or simply, the Atomic Christ. The people of Sedona were ready for surrealism in paintings, but not for crucifix under which Sedona's daily masses were celebrated. Some People made controversial public statements; some adore the Christ sculpture and others despise it. Marguerite had enough of the gossip especially after the one night, when she had the dream of the Atomic Christ, and she confessed to her friend that what came to her dream was not what is usually envisioned as the Christ figure. Marguerite one day decided to drive from Los Angeles and take the crucifix down. The Atomic Christ was cut down in several pieces; his legs, arms, and torso were cast down the desert sands, halfway between Sedona and Los Angeles, that is what the "official story" tells. Some said that the flesh of Chapel's Atomic Christ was buried somewhere around the Chapel's grounds. Either way, only the head of the Atomic Christ had been cut off and was given to Marguerite friend who told Marguerite once, if that fateful day ever does come, and Marguerite decides to take the sculpture down, her best friend would like to keep the head. The Atomic Christ's head, years after Marguerite had passed and her friend died, got missing never to be found after and the Chapel is never to be the same again. The statue displayed today in the Chapel of the Holy Cross is the masterpiece made by famous artist John Muir found to be more traditional. The original sculpture of the Christ of the Atomic Age was crafted by artist Keith Monroe with guidance of sculptress Marguerite Staude. Today, only two photographs posted on the internet have survived, which remind people the Christ of the Atomic Age ever existed.

Cow Pies

Cow Pies is the red rock vortex formation in the close proximity to the Sedona center. Many decades ago Cow Pies became a gathering site for meditation practitioners and hikers. The cow pies look-alike formation, is first observed by the Pioneers and Sinagua alike, since Cow Pies is on the historical trail connecting Sedona and Flagstaff areas. Cow Pies could be part of the historical Palatkwapi Trail, but any solid historical evidence is lacking. Jesse W. Fewkes concluded that based on the ethnographic evidence found, the main Palatkwapi trail must have been located along the Wet Beaver Creek, which is connecting today's Jerome and Winslow via Sedona, however, this could be just one of its side roads. The Munds Wagon Trail started as the quest of rancher Jim Mund to improve it, and was the main cattle road for the Pioneer period after 1896, was completed by the Sedona pioneer Thompson, founder of Coconino County, in 1902. The Road's name today is Schnebly Hill Road. The Mund's Wagon

Trail was also called the Munds Road in the pioneer time. Today, the Munds Wagon Trail is a favorite trail for many mountain bikers from all over the country, and the trail starts from the Schnebly Hill parking lot, leads up to the hill for some four miles, pass Cow Pies, and Merry-Goes-Around rock formation, and ends at the Carousel Rock formation with interesting outcroppings , named donkey and elephant. The trail continues further into Sedona wilderness until it reaches a peak with sweeping views of Sedona, Mitten Ridge, and the Mund Mountain wilderness. The Munds Trail has been voted as one of the best trails in the entire country and is the best-kept secret of the mountain bikers, and since the Munds Road is a less traveled, since the 1930s when cattle-raising faded away. Recently the U.S. Forest Service restored this trail making it easy to climb, but it is still a dirt road. From the intersection "Y", take the 179a south 0.3 miles, and on the next round bound to take the Schnebly Road to the left for 0.9 miles until you reach the Schnebly Hill parking lot. From this point the road is made for all-wheel-drive cars but if you decide to take a hike, it would take four miles to reach the carousel rock formation, which is the official end of the trail. Left on the trail you should take turn to the Cow Pies Rock formation, and the Cow Pies vortex is located on the top of the rock. Cow Pies are 3 circular rock formations which look like cow pies from the air. The top of Cow Pies does have rocks arranged in the medicine wheel circular alignments and is frequently visited by the locals as a favorite spot for meditation. The Medicine Wheel is the Plain's Indian tradition, and has nothing to do with the local Yavapai-Apache tribe, nor with the Pueblo Hopi to the north of the City of Sedona. This Medicine Wheel is arranged by the New Age practitioners frequently visiting Cow Pies. From this spot, the magnificent view spreads around the Mingus Mountain, Mitten Ridge, and ends at the Steamboat Rock. Cow Pies from far distance has a smooth and polished surface, but standing on the top of the rock, many grooves are visible with their cuts going through the rock, forming the Cow Pies' unique shape.

Airport Vortex

Airport vortex is the most visited Sedona Vortex location due to its close proximity to Uptown Sedona, its Airport, and very populated and desirable area of West Sedona. From the "Y", take 89A south and make a turn to the Airport Rd. to your left. Some half mile up to the Airport Road take the first parking lot to the left of the road, which leads up to the Airport Vortex Mesa. The hike is an easy few hundred feet up the hill to your left side. Once you reach the top of the Airport Mesa, the epicenter of its strong vortex energy is on the two adjoined oval rocks on the top of the Airport Mesa Vortex rock formation. Popular vista offers 360-degrees sweeping views of the whole Sedona area, its surrounding rocky hills and the whole Verde Valley to the south with a wide endless horizon. The Airport Vortex is described as the up-flow vortex, masculine vortex with the strong feel electric uplifting geomagnetic energy that does strengthen your own confidence and your masculine side, if you are a man or it will balance your feminine side if you are a woman. You will be able to observe several old Juniper trees that are swirled due to the growth in the center of the vortex. This location is one of the most popular spots for taking photographs. The one lucky enough to find empty parking spot, usually at dawn, will find that this Vortex is a perfect spot for balancing the second chakra or the orange chakra which is located just below the navel and is responsible for everything that is reproductive, including creativity in every aspect of one's life. One such technique, which involves strengthening the body is to stand in upright position with legs slightly spread out their waist length and hands positioned on the love handles. Take a deep breath and inhale it with a 180 degree body rotation cycle and then exhale when your pelvis rotates forward for another 180-degree cycle. This technique helps balance the feminine side, and the weak feminine side signs do involve coldness, depression, low mental energy, slow digestion. One quick check whether you have a feminine or a masculine side prevalent in your body, and which one is more dominant for you, is closing right nostril with the thumb and in turn, closing left nostril while taking your deep breath. If your left nostril is more open for inhaling air, then your feminine side is more dominant, and if your right nostril is easier for inhaling air, then it is your masculine side that is prevailing in your body. The strengthening of masculine side is important for making life decisions with self-confidence, which do involve the reason and it is also crucial to build one masculine side strong, whether you are a woman or a man. The masculine side weakness involves quick temper, releasing excessive body heat with body itch and dryness, excessive appetite, sexual energy, or blocked right nostril. The Airport Mesa Vortex is known as the uplifting or the "upflow" vortex that does release or uplift the body and spirit.

Wind Tunnels

Wind Tunnels or Wind Caves are least traveled, yet very accessible vortex sites in Sedona. Located at the 34.841933-111.776423 GPS position approach from the "Y" south on 179A highway, passed the Oak Creek Cliffs Dr. and Poco Diablo Resort the small turn will be on your right side. If you see Mallard drive, you probably passed it and you need to turn back. The Oak Creek Cliffs located above the Chavez Crossing Campground and the Oak Creek that flows below, provide a great photography scenery year-round. The Wind Tunnels Cave is a short hike down on its well-established trail and the most significant fact, as their name tells, is that the Tunnels are carved by winds, not by the water below. The wind tunnels are small and easy to explore natural shelter from the outside elements that provide the year-round, almost perfect temperature. Since, Wind Tunnels were the favorite spot for Sinagua and today older residents of Sedona doremember the Caves were filled with pottery shards, which are now long time gone. It is very well documented that breaking of the pottery dishes is used in the sacred rituals throughout the American Southwest and this practice was very common across their cultural boundaries prior to the Spanish arrival, just as the Kachina Cult had been widespread throughout the Pueblo world after 1300 to the day. Little is known how and why these religious rituals were performed, since there were no written records or oral history preserved to this day. The pottery with a hole drilled at their button was found in the burial sites of the ancient Pueblos, and where dish was put over the face of the deceased. The hole at the bottom of the dish is supposed to be an inner portal tunnel, between the bodies which represent the underworld, and their souls that were entering heaven through this open portal. What is very significant in breaking dishes on sacred, locations will never be fully understood and we can only speculate about it. The consensus was made among most of today's American anthropologists and the archaeologists that there was a major shift in most religious practices right around 1300, which is supported by the archeological evidence of migrations and abandonment of this period. While there are numerous theories how the Sinagua religion has changed, the arrival of the early Kachina Cult corresponds with the Sinagua departure from the Sedona area between 1330 to 1400 A.D. While the Wind Tunnels were the sacred location for Sedona Sinagua, the actual vortex geomagnetic energy is located on mound, a short distance walk from Wind Tunnels with three vortex swirled Juniper Trees on the top. There is a giant boulder below the Juniper Tree that emits the strongest geomagnetic energy. Many meditators claim that the Wind Tunnels Vortex in emanates the most balanced energy that one can experience. The boulder is very well positioned to face the West, and it is a great location for watching sunsets and taking souvenir photos since it has its swirled Juniper trees and Red Sedona Rocks in its background.

Soldier Pass, Devil's Kitchen, Seven Sacred Pools

Forest Service Trail 66 is the Sedona visitors and residents favorite trail and it could be accessed from West Sedona via 179A from the "Y" and turning right on the Soldier Pass Road. Parking lot position is at GPS 34 53'03.4" N 111 47'01.8" W. Parking lot is very small, and it can accommodate only fourteen vehicles, and parking is not allowed along the roadside. Therefore, it is recommended to come early, the parking lot is open from 08:00 am-06:00 pm. Alternative parking is also available coming from Uptown Sedona to Jordan's Trail. From the Soldier Pass Parking lot, the trail goes for a round loop that is 4.2 miles long and it takes approximately 2.5 hours to hike. Horseback riding is allowed for most of the trail, and with no bicycle rides in the wilderness area. A bicycle ride is allowed only for the first 1.3 miles and The Soldier Pass Trail will lead you to an unusual rock formation named Sphinx Rock, visible right after you leave the parking lot. A quarter-mile from the Soldier Pass parking lot and after crossing a dry creek bed you reach the active sinkhole named the Devil's Kitchen, located halfway on the trail. Sedona's geologist Paul Lindberg thinks that the Devil's Kitchen sinkhole is unique in its creation, and unlike the sinkhole that forms in erosion of limestone caverns, in Sedona's Devil Kitchen limestone is never present. The Devil's Kitchen was created by the collapse of a very large rock cavern into the underground river, which brings the water from Flagstaff. The San Francisco Peak rivers begin under Sedona and Verde Valley end deep below the Tuzigoot Monument, which is the largest Sinagua town ever made. The San Francisco Peaks is the sacred mountain for the Natives of Arizona. In the Palatkwapi's story, the Hopi legend talks about the underworld with rivers below, and the rise of the Great Water Serpent at the closing of their Third World. How large are these caverns and how many of these caverns there are in the Sedona area, nobody knows but it is speculated they cover most of the Red Rock country. Some half way hike from the Devil's Kitchen, you will find the Seven Sacred Pools.

Indian Gardens and Oak Creek Canyon

Indian Gardens is the location where this modern story of Sedona has begun. Some four miles from exiting Uptown Sedona you will see the Indian Gardens Market sign to your left side. Right across the Indian Gardens Market is the landmark plaque that is dedicated to modern town of Sedona and this is the spot where Jim Thompson built his first cabin not having the slightest idea that his garden will become landmark and one of the most visited areas for people from the greater Phoenix area in a hot summer months and international vortex hunters. Just below the Indian Garden's stone landmark, on the right side of the creek bed is a less known vortex site. The Oak Creek Vortex location was first mentioned in original Page Bryant vision, the metaphysical manifestation in her first dream of person named Albion, who initially revealed the vortexes to Page Bryant, namely; the Boynton Canyon, Airport Mesa, Bell Rock, Red Rock Crossing, Indian Gardens and the U.S. Post Office rock in Uptown

Sedona. Over time, more locations emerged as the people from all around the World poured in Sedona, and in the days of the famous Harmonic Convergence in 1986, many more new vortex locations have been reported. The Oak Creek Vortex at the Indian Gardens is characterized as the "In Flow" vortex where the negative energies are absorbed or washed away down the Oak Creek stream.Second Oak Creek Canyon Vortex is located at 4401Old Indian Road what is now the location of the bed and breakfast,"Your Heart's Home". The third known vortex in the Oak Creek Canyon is located fifteen miles from Uptown Sedona toward Flagstaff, after the switchbacks. Look for the Indian Craft Market at the Vista Point, and when you park walk toward the Vista Overlook. The Vista Overlook Vortex is located at the very end of the Vista Overlook, where you can see the Canyon below. The Oak Creek Canyon Overlook is described as the "Upflow" or "Lateral Combination Vortex". The U.S. Post Office vortex revealed by Albion to Page Bryant is located right on the "Y" center location, where the highways 89A and 179 A merge.

West Fork Trail Vortex

West Fork Trail is a magnificent trail and probably one of the most scenic trails in the United States. Oak Creek Canyon itself is voted one of the five most scenic roads in North America, and West Fork Trail is a part of this biodiverse system in the American Southwest. West Fork Trail runs for more than fourteen miles deep, however, only the first three miles is recommended for hiking, since the trail is not developed after, and is today considered the most untouched and pristine clean wilderness. West Fork Trail has the Parking fee area which is located eleven miles north on 89A from the Uptown toward Flagstaff, one mile north passed the Don Hoel's Cabin and left of the roadmark 384. West Fork Trail starts from the southwest corner of the parking lot where famous Mayhew Lodge ruin is still visible. From the parking lot the trail will take you west passing the old apple orchard that is home to an old German apple tree that is now extinct in their old native country. The ruin of the Mayhew's

Lodge, which was a vacation home to many Hollywood celebrities prior to the great fire that buried the glorious history of Sedona, the home to more than 200 western movies is now taken over by nature. In the late 1800s, the first hunter who settled down in the West Fork Creek and built his first cabin was known to locals as Bear Howard, He got his nickname after hunting for Grizzly Bears, legends say, sometimes only with a knife. Howard had a personal vendetta with bears after his friend had been mauled to death. Howard eventually stopped after he killed the last bear in the Oak Creek Canyon. The other families followed, and eventually, the Flagstaff photographer Carl Mayhew came to work on the film based on Zane Grey's novel "Call of the Canyon". Mayhew built his new Lodge that opened for the guests in 1926 and many Hollywood stars followed, including; Jimmy Stewart, Clark Gable, Walt Disney, even President Herbert Hoover. The lodge has been open until 1968, when the Mayhew's family sold it to the U.S. Forest Service for historical purpose and because of the unfortunate fire in 1980, the Lodge went down and is in ruins ever since. The West Fork Trail is the easiest longest trail in Sedona and the most beautiful one. It has thirteen creek crossings along three miles and some of them have to be crossed on foot and sometimes with its water up to the knees. The West Fork Trail is the home to less known "outflow" or "lateral vortex", located under the huge boulder in the middle of the Creek with the small tree growing out of the boulder. This boulder is located approximately a half-way throughout the trail. The West Fork vortex is outflow lateral vortex, and is recommended for the solitary meditation with the intention of "letting go" the worries, strings and burdens that accumulated in the soul or mind over time. Many miles of the underground caverns and shafts are leftovers from past volcanic eruptions, with underground rivers running through them. The underground river systems are all fortified by geomagnetic energy produced by the Sedona's iron-rich soil and the quartz crystals embedded in sandstone will do their job.

Broken Arrow, Devil's Dining Room, Submarine Rock and Chicken Point

From the "Y" intersection of the roads SR 179, and SR 89A, drive southeast on SR 179 for 3.6 miles. Turn left to Morgan Road, and sign the parking area. The Broken Arrow trail can be accessed from the Chapel Road or the Little Horse trailhead, however, to make a hike short and access the Chicken Point vortex, quick and easy, the trail should be reached via Morgan Road. The whole loop hike is 4.8 miles, but if the Submarine Rock trail spur is taken, the length of 1.5 miles is added to the total length. The Broken Arrow Trail is lengthy, scenic, rewarding and it ends at the Chicken Point Vortex site. Have you decided to take the Pink Jeep Tours, you will have a wild ride with a stop at the Devil's Dining Room sinkhole which is one of the major seven sinkholes in the Sedona area. The Devil's Dining Room sinkhole is marked and fenced with a barbed-wire fence. The Pink Jeep tour stops first at the Submarine Rock and at its end, the Chicken Point, as well as, at the hiking trail, however, hiking this trail is a completely different kind of experience, and a more rewarding one. Extend your hike with outstanding views, and your hike should start at the Chapel of the Holy Cross parking lot, including visit to the Chapel as well, with its short loop around the Twin Buttes. The Broken Arrow Trail got its name after the famous movie "The Broken Arrow" made in 1950, starring Jimmy Stewart. The Chicken Point offers the most beautiful vistas of Sedona and its small rock formation is home to Sedona's frequently visited vortex. The Twin Nuns can be seen at the start of this trail, as well as, the "Eagle Rock". The trail goes around the Twin Buttes and ascends to the end of the trail, and this is the Chicken Point with its small, red rock formation that is the epicenter of vortex. There is a sweeping view from the Chicken Point and its Vortex which covers the most beautiful views of the Valley below and to it's north, up from this point. The Chicken Point Rock is a great spot for solitary morning meditation, since you will be hyperventilated after the steep climb.

Bradshaw Ranch

Among many Sedona attractions is the UFO Museum located at the Center for the New Age, 341 State Route 179, Sedona, AZ 86336. The store offers the UFO tour with military-grade night goggles and visits the most reported UFO sites around the town. People that are reporting UFO Sedona occurrences are numbered in thousands for the last four decades and the Native American stories of visitation by the Sky People are dating back to the ancient times. Most UFO sight-seeings were reported around the Bell Rock and forgotten site of the Bradshaw Ranch. The ranch is located between Honanki and Palatki Heritage sites on the forest road 525c going toward Honanki on North Loy Butte Road (525c), turn left on the Red Canyon Road. The Bradshaw Ranch has been overnight purchased by the Federal Government and is closed to the public. According to MUFON; the Mutual UFO network reporting archives, Arizona is one of three top active UFO states and Bradshaw Ranch has a special place. This is, perhaps, not the UFO visiting site, but a gateway for the criss-cross dimensional travel, where the souls can breach into the future or the past. The new theory has been introduced, in which UFO visitations are not alien visitations, but human ones, visiting us from the future and past. This new way of thinking should fit well into the Native American souls' migration legends, and Albert Einstein time travel theory, and with is coexistence of the multiple dimensions. Another interesting fact is that the seven canyons converge in this area, and USGS confirms that Sedona has a very high level of geomagnetic activity, one highest in the area. The very high UFO activity began in 1992, when Bob Bradshaw's wife Linda woke up by the strange loud noise activity around 3 A.M. and from there on she started to catalog the events. Many old TV crews visited the ranch and filmed the strange activities in the sky, which includes the appearance of a white strange orbs, that are reported around Sedona. The MUFON researcher Tom Dongo documented all the activities in his book the "Merging Dimensions".

Seven Canyons

The Seven Canyons enclose a cluster of north of Palatki, Honanki and Bradshaw Ranch triangle. The least traveled canyon in Sedona is Sycamore Canyon, which is the part of Coconino Wilderness and is a home to Sycamore Creek, which is four times larger than Oak Creek and output pristine clear water that is drinkable at its source. Sycamore Canyon is the first area in Arizona that was set aside as wilderness area and is the largest canyon among the seven canyon area that converge here. Sycamore Canyon is 21 miles long and 23 miles wide located west of the "Y"center of Uptown Sedona. The Parson's Trail in Sycamore Canyon starts in Cottonwood, is a four miles long, one way. From Cottonwood take north through Old Town Cottonwood for two miles, turn east, with a right turn at the first Tuzigoot turnoff. From this place, continue drive some half a mile to 131 Sycamore Canyon Road., and drive 6.7 miles to the North, take a left turn at the fork for another 3 miles until you can reach the trailhead parking lot. The trail follows Sycamore Creek for four miles and is full of a Juniper, Pinon, and tall Cypress trees along the red rocks and naturally formed pools among them. Some hikers do spend the night in the canyon, often by using old rancher Nick Perkins cabin, which is registered on the National List of the Historic Places as an old overnight shelter. Forest Service rangers are concerned about people who leave their food behind, attracting the Black Bears, which often end up with the Black Bear being put down for people safety. East of Sedona's Sycamore Canyon is Loy Canyon and it's trailhead sits on the same road heading to Honanki, just a mile before Honanki. Loy Canyon has Indian Ruins and three of them alongside the trail itself. Take 89A and turn right on Forest Rd. 525, stay on the road until you reach the trailhead parking lot. GPS is 34.55'56.29" N, and 111.55'30. 15" W. Continue to upper Loy Canyon Butte, which is the highest peak and you will see the three ruins, and you will be rewarded with smaller cliff dwellings.

Application

Native Americans insist that whole Sedona and Verde Valley is one giant vortex, while most of the New Age Movement, which is very diverse and can not be confined to only one group with the specific beliefs, insist on a many smaller locations, four, five, seven or even many hundred, depends on whom you are talking to. The truth must have been somewhere in between, the question arises are there any known scientific data that will confirm the Sedona exceptionalism in the wide American Southwest, and perhaps in the whole World. The answer is absolutely and categorical, yes. Since the early 1980 some speculations came out of Sedona about this, particularly after 1987 that is the year of Great Harmonic Convergence, resulting in Sedona being in the international spotlight. On that fateful day, the traffic was more than a nightmare in Sedona and along 179A and 89A highways. The hotel rooms were packed up and there were even people sleeping out. The main event has occurred at the Bell

Rock and the Spaceship Rock plateau, where about two thousand individuals or so gathered and there was rumor of people dancing naked around Baby Bell and even the Spaceship's boarding passes were sold on the street. There was a rumor that the Space Ship will be coming to town to take the people on the ride. There was even a rumor the human sacrifice happened at the Apache Leap, when the Apache refused to surrender to the U.S. Calvary, eventually having thrown themselves off the cliffs to avoid the arrest. This historical event happened one century earlier, but the real location was at the Superstitions Mountains, east of today's Phoenix. In a mass event, everything may happen, when even those wildest rumors become reality. The exodus of Yavapai-Apache in Verde Valley happened, but it was an orderly event, with casualties on the way to the San Carlos Reservation. There was no mass sacrifice, nobody has been thrown off the Apache Leap Cliffs, and Spaceships did not arrive, and there is no photo evidence of naked dance, but sociologically it was a very important event that shows the American generation of Hippies and Baby Boomers had the need to reinvent themselves, and they surely did. The New Age soul found itself, perhaps, not in an orderly way, but surely secured the future of this new movement that represents some 64 million followers worldwide. The New Age Movement is not built as the organized religion, but is much more the movement that has its roots in rebellious sixties, and is based on love, empathy, charity, and openness to the point that is one of the most diverse movements in the World and unlike the World Bodies such as United Nations, has no hierarchy and no doctrine. The New Age movement has no ideology, no religion, no race, no creed or ethnicity, however, it embraces all the above. The one can think of the New Age as being open to everybody and the one can conclude that the New Age is, if not the most open community in the World, a microcosm of the American Society. The Harmonic Convergence was not an orderly event and rumors harm the New Age movement and community of Sedona, however, this was the most significant event that marked the end of an Era and the start of a new one.

The damage was done to the relationship of the Native American

communities and the New Age followers where there was a silent

animosity going on between the New Age Movement, and Native

American tribes. The animosity is heading only in one direction,

from the Native Americans toward the New Age practitioners for

doing rituals on the Native American Sacred grounds, which did

include Sedona. The New Age Convergence gatherings happened

on the other locations, in particular in the Chaco Canyon Culture,

where the New Age ceremonies and rituals were done, on the sites

of the ancient Anasazi people. This was a sacrilege for the Native

American tribes, since such ceremonies were performed on sacred

grounds, whether they involve burial sites or not. Since the 1980s,

regulations have changed and even for a simple short archeological

survey on reservation or Native American sacred ground the permit

is needed for the group other than the local tribe. On the other hand,

the New Age followers do not hold any grudge toward the Native

American Culture, on contrary they embrace it, and they do not see anything wrong with their visitations, ceremonies or rituals done in open. The other possible harm the 1987 Harmonic Convergence did to the town and to people of Sedona, unintentionally is to expose an ill intention of some people in which they ridicule, dismiss or harm in any possible way the Native American heritage or the New Age movement and supposed hoax of vortex sites. The next two decades were marked by all negative attitudes, until someone decided to use the scientific method, with all the measurements. In the early 2000, Sedona engineer Benjamin Lonetree began his pioneering scientific studies, together with local artist, and the Sedona's hypnotherapist, Ionna Miller, which has been summarized in their co-work named, "The Sedona Effect". Benjamin Lonetree was the first and the only scientist that employed the scientific study into the Sedona's vortex phenomena and came with positive results. Lonetree's flux meters/ gauss measurement came with undeniable electromagnetic and the geomagnetic numbers that showed the vortex energy. The Vortex plume exists and can be measured, this was the message that came from the Lonetree studies, and he finally put to rest all the previous popular debates and speculations. Other such groups followed with the support of the TV crews and Gene got out of the bottle. All of a sudden the people of Sedona have the hard final scientific evidence supporting the Vortex theory. Benjamin Lonetree has had his study supported by the map of the USGS, that is readily available on the government web sites, with the clear resolution color-coded photos in known aerial surveillance of the American Southwest, surely the maps are not saying Vortex, but are showing the major geomagnetic disturbances through the state of Arizona with Sedona in its clear red-hot spot. Furthermore, Ben Lonetree studies called upon the lab studies of Canadian doctor Michael Persinger that involved studies of direct effects of the magnets on the human psyche, behavior, and the healing methods of the geomagnetic field in his clinical trials of epilepsy and many other medical conditions. The question remains, What are the real applications of conducted studies on the possible psychic harvesting of the Sedona natural geomagnetic field from a scientific perspective and what better place is to be, since there are thousands of psychics and mediums in Sedona, contributing with their skills and with yours, soon. The scientific community accepts data in the most controlled laboratory environment with a hundred percent data's accuracy and precision, and open Sedona lab has the problem that Mother Nature controls the data, and its timing. This vortex plume depends on many factors; like the time of year, solar flares, the Moon Cycles, and many other factors which affects the individual psychic ability that could rise at the particular vortex in the given specific time. On the other hand, the majority of psychics don't need a data evidence, they already have it. The public is left in between, to believe it or not to believe it, after all, everything is based on a belief system. The Native American community do not need evidence either, but if presented with scientific numbers, will say that they knew about that and will ask you why the white men are so persistent in disbelief. So far, we ended up with the numbers and validated data, which are ignored by the scientific community, and are left with even more confused public. The most usual answer

from psychic is always, " We can use it!" The locations of the most

significant Sedona vortexes are well-known and with preparation, it

is easy work to harvest vortex energy. There is a catch, the one has

to believe, not in the vortex, but in its own ability to go through the

portal of time to another dimension, not with body, but with mind,

Sedona vortex is only there to amplify and to bridge space and time.

After the belief comes the wish, the wish to connect with the loved

ones, the One's wish to bridge physical separation of time between

the living in this Earth's dimension and living on the other side. The

stronger is the belief in the system that is amplified by strong wish,

and be in the right place at the right time, the technicality of such

psychic work will become, as easy as, the first baby steps. Natural

side of such meditation practices and preparations involves food

chemistry such as spinach or pumpkin seeds. Mother Nature is at

play, that involves major solar cycles, where the magnetic fields

are the most active during the spring and fall equinoxes in March

20-21 st, and September 20- 21st, and to a lesser extent during the winter solstice, December 20-21st with least vibrations during the summer solstice, June 21st. The time of a day does make difference and during melatonin's peak secretion time, from Dusk until Dawn and around two a.m., when the melatonin secretion is culminating. The lunar cycle has played a role in the Native American rituals for thousands of years. Sinagua did solar archeo-astronomy viewings and proof is found in V-Bar-V and in Palatki so far, but evidence of the Lunar Cycle observation is lacking in Sedona, for now. What we know so far, the lunar cycle plays a key role in human behavior and on the full moon nights, the psychic abilities are amplified.

Preparation

Like in any physical and mental work, whether it is the marathon or simple school test, psychic work ahead of you requires preparation. Working with the vortex energy requires just that, with a difference, it requires subconscious, not conscious preparations. The technique is actually easier to start with, although our rational mind says no to the subconscious thinking and there is less required preparation for the incoming subconscious work and it could be, as easy as, dream and dreaming. A dream is nothing else but the one's altered state of awareness, in which our conscious and rational mind is put to rest. A dream with many mystical, fantastic, and symbolic occurrences may happen and that is almost always disregarded as a part of the fantasy of dreams. Most people take the dreams as, no more than the daytime entertainment, like a movie that is made just for that, just entertainment and if you are one of them, you are wasting the precious time and Sedona was not meant to be for you. It was just romantic three-day weekend with great scenery and entertainment.

On the contrary, if you do believe in the power of your dreams, and if you remember them vividly, if some of them turn to reality in the days to come, and if you are sure there has been something seen in your dream, which you can tame it, and use it to predict your future and change your own destiny, Sedona is for you. Many people own their "dream catcher", hanging in their car's mirror, and this is not just the statement of affiliation with Native American community. The symbolism of dream catcher is reminder to the person willing to have an open mind, catch and control their dreams. The symbol is a frequent daily subconscious reminder of the inner willingness to leave their subconscious open at all times. After all, how much time we spent in our cars and beds and if we have the small dream catcher that hung over a bed. This could be the constant night and morning reminder of our openness to interpret our future and past. This is just a small symbolic step in the preparation of the psychic work ahead and the pledge that I can and will do it, and that I can, because I know that it is there, it has always been there. Your own dream is the muffler of the soul, your deep reminder of your daily life, your past and your future. Think, the dream is the backyard or the patio that you have. Think, is your backyard neglected and have you cleaned it up or is your backyard in the perfect condition and needs only a daily brush up. Your backyard is exactly that, the physical projection of the condition of your soul's backyard, with your relation to it. Stop now, and drop down everything you do, at this very moment, ask yourself what are the feelings that are going through you right now? What is the condition of the soul backyard, think of your feelings at this very moment, and find out do you feel angry, guilty, sorry or you feel proud, self-satisfied, self-motivated. The feeling at this moment is; what you think about and how you visualize your backyard, does feeling tell you anything about the relationship with your soul, and your deep self, and what you want to do with it. Two-thirds of people who came to this town say they visited a local psychic to find the answer, what lays ahead for them?

Dream

Have you ever heard of anyone cheerfully going to the hospital or school, whether it is a student or a teacher, a physician or a patient? The same is partially true with a psychic visit because unlike you, who is in a rush, need to know the outcome of the reading, whether it is about love, health or the business decision related reading, your psychic will be a very calm and worry-free. Unlike the students that worry about the test or the grade, or the patient worry about the lab and x-ray results, and unlike the teacher or doctor that worry about coming to work late and their reputation at all times, the psychic is calm and relaxed. Psychic always knows the outcome and because psychic controls the timeline and knows irrelevant of the illusion of time. The Psychic's knowledge and abilities are as important as the knowledge and the abilities of the elementary school teacher or the high university institution professor. There is only one difference, and just like with any other profession, the knowledge and personal ability make the difference and curb the outcome of your reading. Like in any other craft, the talent is ten percent and the hard work is ninety percent, therefore, you are the psychic even if you are at only one percent, that one is very important. The question is, are willing to take the remaining ninety-nine percent of the hard labor? As You will find out, it is very easy task, if you put a lot of faith in it, and a dream is the very first exercise to work on, partially because we are all familiar with dreams and their interpretation, and partially we all had the hunch experience of the vivid dream come through, at least once in the lifetime. The dream interpretation has been popularized so much in the public life of western society in the past centuries, that we are all open to it and prompted ahead of time to accept the possibility of the dream come through. Our inner predisposition to accept our dream's meaning and the precognitive dream realization in the future makes work with dreams the easiest path toward the bridging space and time. Even most Sedona's vortex skeptics will not deny that they had a dream come through in their lifetime, at least once. Taking the notebook next to the nightstand is the first course of action with expectancy that the vivid dream might come that night or in a several nights ahead. You can not make an active invocation of the events, calling the event or person to show up in our dreams, it takes years of hard work. What we can do when we start remembering and interpreting our own dreams, is to block our rational mind which makes the expectations, and rational thinking blocked or for an even better word, ignore. Ignoring the dream that we do expect tonight, and let it come when the dream pleases would be the best course of action. This way we let the subconscious mind be open without a projected timeline. The Paradox is, by blocking the scientific rational mind and sorting things up this way we let the dream come through, but that is the way what this craft is all about, and how the subconsciousness works. This can not be put in the lab tube and controlled, try to do that, you will surely fail. Success does require an attitude of, "Letting it go!" Having a light dinner or even skipping dinner altogether is the first course of business. Second is to have tea before sleep,can be chamomile or any other calming tea.

Expect to have a great long sleep without possible interruptions and

do not think that the dream will happen that night. When it does, no

matter how vivid or odd a dream comes through, try not to open the

eyes right away, repeat the main scene of the dream with eyes shut.

The processor filtrates these main scenes, like movie scenes several

times if possible. You are waking up, and at this moment, you want

to catch the dream because your conscious mind is waking up and

your subconscious mind is pushed away. This moment is crucial so

much that you want to use the pencil and paper on your nightstand.

It may take several weeks, or even a month before this becomes the

fun routine of catching dreams. The sole anticipation of this future

remembrance of their dream will only push up the subconscious by

conscious like the teacher asking students to repeat the homework.

Both sides have the anticipation of the outcome of that task and the

conscious self or subconscious self are ready for their homework.

This tune may not happen on the first night, just like the chemistry of love does not happen on the first date, but it will somehow take a place. Sometimes, it could take whole month and this depends on the belief in self and the inner psychic sense, which we possess. The more inner self-confidence you have in yourself with a small vortex gift of Mother Nature, the easier psychic work will be. Remember, incoming dreams is the first step to the interpretation of your future precognitive dreams and with a lot of meditation practice ultimately toward your lucid dream or daydream, where you will be aware of your dream and to a lesser extent of your surroundings. This lucid dream or what is sometimes called the astral dream is the first step in your long journey and you will be able to catch and control your dream, because it often has flying sensation, which is called Astral. The inner sensation may often result in the out-of-body experience, when your inner self leaves your body and quite often elevates self above your body. Do not get scared, you do not have to get to this level in order to be able to interpret the dreams or to have the vivid precognitive dreams of future events. The focus and persistence of the dream journal is the most important work that you can do before coming to Sedona for a vortex experience that will help. Motivation to have precognitive dream is very important and the dream book at your nightstand is friendly reminder of the dream journey that will follow and the easiest thing you can do to prompt subconscious and your inner self to see the future or the past. The average REM cycle is about two hours, and if you have noticed, sometimes you will be more rested after the six hours of sleep, than seven and a half. The reason is that you have caught three REM cycles in each case since the brain recognizes full REM within two hours cycle. When your last dream cycle is cut short by waking up, the brain will recognize only the first completed deep three REM cycles and if you had the precognitive dream of the event that will happen in the future at the first moment you will not remember it, but if you do, use the dream notebook you will find it. This excitement that would prompt your subconscious to work harder with your dream and expect the future events. Sometimes your precognitive dream will be very vivid and will involve the people that you will recognize, places and events that you are familiar with, and sometimes it could be harder since there are the symbols and all fantastic events that you have to sort through. As you become very good with remembering and sorting all through your dreams, you will be able to make an interpretation of the unknown personalities, the people and events that you have never seen before because your own conscious will be prepared to recognize that these are future events and persons. As you become the master of your dreams, when even the most fantastic and unreal events, people and places in your dreams will suddenly become the most important details to sort through, and after all, these events of the future may be even life-saving. Your conscious or the inner soul will master your dream, like you master driving skills, throughout your life.

Remembering the dream

Remembering the dream is the first and hardest skill you can train yourself. When we start waking from our sleep, in this semi-awake state, this is the crucial moment where we have to hold the dream, literally, catch it by both sides, start and the end of the dream, and with closed eyes strive to grab the dream notebook from nightstand. At first, this will be very hard to do, because the wakening up is that very moment, in the seconds where our subconscious mind is going to sleep, and the conscious mind is awakening from its sleep. This is, as easy as, being in the awake state, and leaving the room full of the people and furniture we have never seen before, notice them all in that room we have just passed through for that moment. Closing the door behind you and exiting the room, you will encounter your awakened conscious self that asks your subconscious self, "What is that you have seen in that room that you just left?" You were not told before entering this room to remember the things, people and events, right? That is how hard it is to try to remember the dreams that we are not tuned to, or expect it. Well, what if you are told by someone, say your inner self, to remember everything, which you have seen in that room and that there will be the school test of what you could remember after exit, would be much easier, right? What if you try to repeat the process of entering the unknown room, and remember everything you have seen, and hold those memories after the exit for the incoming written test? This will be simple since you are predisposed to it, pre-trained, and expect it. This is exactly what happens with your dream notebook, the diary of your dreams put to work. The more you practice and master your inner knowledge of communicating the information acquired by your subconscious self in a dream state, the more ability you have in your conscious self at that moment of waking up to catch, hold and remember information until you write it down. Your dream notebook is the most important tool that you need in your psychic training with your persistence to push all your limits, and above all, the belief in yourself.

Interpretation of dreams

Your dream can come vivid with the known people and the known surroundings, with the unknown people and places, or what is more common, with symbolism involves the mythical places, creatures or events. It seems that it doesn't matter in what form the dream comes to you, the hardest part is their interpretation. Numerous books have been written on the interpretation of dreams, summarizing them in common patterns recognizable to everyone. These common human interpretative patterns of the dreams recognition have cross-cultural symbolic meanings universal for all humanity, but the details of this hidden message are understandable only to the dreamer, even when the dreamer could not consciously understand it. The dreamer has to analyze its own dream in full detail with the help of the dream book or the interpretation manual. The analysis is similar to translating a foreign language with the Webster translator. The dreamer finds the common message of the dream, and has to review a few past days and what people or events have influenced the dreamer in the recent past. This could be as simple as a daily review of the people that we meet on a daily basis. When the people or events in their dreams are hard to understand, and when it might be some unknown people or places that come in a dream its dreamer has never seen before, but they have an implication on the dreamer's personal life or affects a dreamer as a part of dreamer's larger social group. For instance, a week before September 11, I had the dream which vividly portrays the ancient Egyptians blowing up the pyramids and I had the clear image of the Pharaoh being mad. The next day I told what I dreamt to my Egyptian friend, whose family came from Egypt in the recent aftermath of the 1967 war, as Coptic Christian refugees and settled in Southern California. Five days after I lost my friend, because my dream communication with him had disturbed him to the point of no recovery. On that morning after the dream, I was not able just to connect the dots, except for the fact that I knew something big was coming. On another occasion right before the Pope's election I had a dream of an old man in his white robes approached me speaking

German. Since, the College of Cardinals was still meeting and this

was all over the news and in my vivid closing dream interpretation

was that the new Pope elected will be the young Austrian candidate

which was favored by the College. These daily news did sway my

dream reading in that direction and my conscious self overlooked

the old gray-haired man which appeared in my dream and made me

accept the young one. I knew something was missing, and upon that

point, nobody even heard of Cardinal Ratzinger among the public,

neither did I, but the vivid image of his old face got stuck with me

in the coming days. Your initial interpretation of your dream should

be free of the news or any interruptions that could lead your reading

in different directions. Writing immediately the most recent dream

after waking up is the key for capturing the message from your own

subconscious mind, fully translating it by conscious awareness and

finally, interpreting the dream. The message could have contained

the review of the past, the message concerning the future or simply messages from your loved ones from the other side. Since modern quantum physic's views the time differently that the time has been traditionally seen, a better description should be the messages from another dimension, since the new theory argues that the time could be a simple illusion and that all these events could be happening all simultaneously in several different dimensions. The explanation fits perfectly with the medium experience and messages from the loved ones which have passed. The eternal soul is sending the message in the present, only from the other side, just from another co-existing dimension. How exactly the Sedona vortex will help in this process is not known yet, several schools of thought exist but several point out to the existence in all these inter-dimensional portals. Sedona's geo-magnetic, inter-dimensional portals have connections between the multidimensional space, its bridging space and time have been witnessed by thousands of Sedona visitors. The most passive dream occurrences took place on every Sedona vortex location, and many different individuals are discovering and reporting the vortex sites.

Since the first five sites have been reported by Page Bryant in 1986 to this day there are dozens and most experts do agree, hundreds of the vortex locations to be found. Everybody agree that Sedona is the one giant vortex with the hundreds of the smaller hot spots. This hot spot turns into the daydream medium experience, similar to the real dream visitations of the loved ones that passed. Be at the right time, in the right vortex, when these plumes of the inflow, outflow, or the lateral side vortex energy, which depends partially on Mother Earth, as well as, spring and fall equinoxes are the right time to visit since all these earth geomagnetic disturbances or vortex spinning are the most active at this time. Being prepared and working on your night dream, and later on with meditation techniques, are surely the right way to prepare for the vortex experience. Taking a nap at the vortex locations is one of the techniques practiced by many vortex visitors, and is one way to harvest the energy for a beginner. These messages that come in a dream, is symbolic union that summarizes the pattern of the messages that are fused into the symbol itself. It is good to be familiarized with the universal symbolism and the messages which are unique for all humanity, and are always repeated throughout the ages. Knowledge of the universal symbol appears in the night of the incoming dream and knowing the symbol meaning is the small first step before reviewing personal implications and many recent events affecting us and our loved ones. Work with the vortex would bring in you the strong need for "letting go" of worries or the people that hurt you. Those situations in which there is a strong need to express forgiveness, the vortexes in Oak Creek Canyon and West Fork Trail will be perfect, since both of them are positioned on a water stream, the lateral stream of water works the best for releasing accumulated negative emotions and experiences. These mediumship experiences can be different depending on gender,and outflow of the masculine energy on the Bell Rock Vortex can work the best for many women. Visiting well-traveled and favorite vortexes for thousands of tourist daily could become a small problem, because one condition for the meditation success practice is the quiet, and peaceful space for it,

Therefore, a vortex visit very early in the morning or late at night will spare you from any noises or other interruptions. Meditations early in the morning or even taking a nap at the vortexes late in the evening, for instance, will help to raise melatonin concentrations during evening hours, and with a proper tryptophan-rich diet will increase the chance of a mediumship experience. Keeping a daily journal, with the intention to receive the reading in Sedona, taking raw pumpkin seeds and spinach prior to the visit, and come at the right time of the day, with the right day of the year will yield the positive result. The faith and persistence of the will is crucial and the first stepping stones in achieving psychic success.

Sanctuary

Developing personal sanctuary for the soul is the second task, after work with the personal dream journal that will help you develop the psychic and personal experience with your vortex site. Your vortex tuning helps you develop a remote connection with the best-chosen working vortex site that you would be able to access from anywhere in the World, at any time you will need the personal safety space for your reading. Egoistic as it may sound, this sanctuary can be similar to a sanctuary of the prophets like; Buddha, Jesus, Mohammad, the cave is where those great religions were initially started. In Sedona, it can be the sanctuary of an unknown prophet, at the Airport Mesa Vortex, Shaman's Cave or the Kachina Woman Rock. Either way, it is meant to be a secluded vortex site, which must be easy accessible only to you and to your psychic work. No other person, nor spiritual entity should be allowed to enter the sanctuary for the simple reason that you will be working with the deepest levels of your inner self, and it could be extremely dangerous just to let somebody access this level. People who do not develop the very deep access route to their deepest level of their soul with full protection of it can risk insanity, therefore, if you are not ready to protect your subconsciousness, do not even try. You are now ready to access it with full responsibility, and you will be rewarded with the unimaginable powers of the mind and the unbreakable power of the will allow you full control of your own destiny and the fruitful happiest life in front of you. The ability is there for you to take, and be able to help others as well, on your only path to embrace the universe and your part in it. This is with a full promise not to abuse your acquired abilities. Sanctuary for the soul already exists for all people, however only the responsible few will be able to reach it, access it at will and harvest its full potential. Those who accidentally tap in sanctuary with ill intentions, even on the outskirts of it, hurt themselves in the form of crossing the sacred boundaries and will end at the dark side of insanity. This sanctuary is your safe house that should not be accessible to everybody else, people or entity, and therefore will provide you with the privacy to work with your rediscovered psychic abilities. This safe house will allow you to tap into psychic self through your third eye, above and beyond, to high universal consciousness or oneness of the universe, where the soul initially belongs to. Make sure you will not share the access to the sanctuary with anyone consciously or subconsciously, and you will be safe. Try to build your psychic safe house with only your imagination in a very slow motion, allow yourself to inspect every small detail of the corners of your safe space. The more times you access your safe space over days of practice, the more quickly you will be able to access it, after a small meditation, and the faster your psychic reading will be, but initially, you must start very slow. When you start building your sanctuary with the Kachina Woman Rock you should, actually visit the site physically and will focus on your surroundings from the moment you parked your car. It actually may take 25-30 minute walk toward the Kachina Woman rock, and try to focus on your trail, do remember every unusual stone, vortex twisted juniper trees, wood beams below, supporting the trail, piles of the rock markings showing the trail. Try to count the steps which you are taking climbing the Vista trail. Reaching the very bottom of the Kachina Women Rock, observe the Rock and try to estimate the number of the steps needed to reach the vortex knob from this point on. Finally, climb the final portion of the trail counting those steps. Once you reach the sign where it says "The trail end", sit down on the rock and take a deep breath. Sit cross-legged and make the spine upright, and close your eyes. Use the meditation pillow or backpack as your back support, sit on it, make sure your knees are at the same level with the base of your spine. Rest your wrists on the knees with the ring fingers closing your thumbs in the closed-circuit. Focus on your deep breath and count up to ten breaths with your deep breath intake and deep release, focus only on the number of breaths and nothing else. When your mind starts to wander, do force back your focus on counting your breaths. Once you reach number ten, start the countdown from ten to one and focus on your breath, counting one number with each breath intake, then exhale slowly. Just try to focus on the synchronization of the inhales and numbers counting. Again, if your mind starts to wander around, focus on your breath counting inhales. Once you reach number zero, open your eyes and observe Verde Valley below. Pay your visit at sunset and begin the meditation right after sunset. At dusk, the lights of Sedona and the surrounding area intermingle with the stars in the sky. With your mind, imagine the lights of Sedona down below, and lights of stars above become one. At this point, the whole universal endless space is your source of the unobstructed information available to you and only you. This is only because you are all alone in your sanctuary and the Kachina Women Rock vortex energy is there below you to help tap into your source. The more you repeat the visits to the Kachina Woman Rock, and repeat this exercise, the more you will get familiar with your new sanctuary and the more you will build your own remote access. You would be able to remotely visit your own sanctuary wherever you are, whenever you need to hide and to access and extract the information you seek. Later on, you would be able to repeat the whole exercise with your eyes open. Visualize your surroundings and every rock around you, the Kachina Woman Rock to your left, and the Child Knob to your right side. Say, you meet someone, and you will be able to find out every answer about that person. What someone thinks or does that person has all good intentions toward you or malicious one? What particular person's true intentions are, and your best correct course of action is in that case. Visualize yourself sitting on the Kachina Woman Rock in the sitting position as you did in the training visits and command your inner mind with the words, " Go to sanctuary!", count ten breaths and you will find your true instant answers to any question.

Christian Meditation

It is important to keep in mind at any time that the faith guide and guard all spiritual and psychic work and the more you put trust in your psychic work, guided with your guardian angel, the quicker and easier your psychic success will be. Not understanding eastern traditions when it comes to psycho-somatic work (mind-body) will result in a limited or no psychic success. Since, in all the Christian prayers and meditations, the body-soma change of positions never has been used, like in known eastern traditions found in Hinduism, Buddhism, Islam, body/mind technique is hard to apply in Christian person for the lack of somatic use during the prayers or meditations. The easiest way to approach the problem question is to find all the answers in the most growing and popular eastern tradition in all the western world today and that is yoga. When I asked my good friend Shiva, a Hindu monk, what he thinks of the fact that many millions of Westerners are practicing yoga today and Shiva's simple answer was;" There is one key element missing, yoga faith." In Hinduism

yoga somatic body positions have all the faith elements connection,

therefore, there are the psychosomatic (spirit-body) relationships at

work, which connects all yoga body positions with a spiritual work,

simultaneously. For western yoga practice this spiritual connection

is either missing or is not fully able to be comprehend. This similar

missing link can be found in Judo practice of western man, where

for the Shinto practitioners practice of Judo has divine connection

and for the average western man Judo is just a sport. Having a tea

for Japanese people has its ritual spiritual meaning and connection

and for Englishmen or Russian this can be a more traditional social

event. We can conclude that it is very hard to work with the chakra

system or any body/mind somatic exercise with the western person,

simply because the spirit-body of the mind-body tradition is lacking

in the historic Christianity or is it? This lost Christianity with spirit

body meditation and prayer does exist in the rich Christian tradition

and is known as Hesychast, which has been long-time forgotten and buried below the church dogma for the last six centuries. Hesychast psychosomatic Christian meditation has always been there, it has been developed in the first four centuries of early Christianity, then was lost in the Middle East in the next six centuries. The Hesychast meditation was revived in the twelfth century and has been declared heretical, finally exterminated by the church officials and is only to survive in lost monastic manuscript of Eastern Rome. Existence of the Hesychastic meditation has been brought to the light and public just recently, as a curious relic of the Christian heresy of the remote past. Unlike known Kundalini meditation and seven chakra system of Hinduism, Hesychast Christian meditation holds on only four of them, associated with the upper parts of the human body and never goes below waist or lower parts of the spine, because of the Nicene Christian view of the original sin and the fall of man. The dogmatic view does not mean that in the early times of the Christian history, the entire human body was not covered with Hesychast prayer, but there is no existing manuscript with any evidence from that time to confirm it. All we have today are surviving manuscripts sometimes contradictory, of the great works left by the Christian theologians, such as the trio; St.Gregory of Palamas, Nikephoros the Hesychast, and St.Gregory of Sinai. The obvious connection with a techniques in Hinduism or Islam and their simultaneous work of the body/soul taking place in the Hesychast meditation prompts some scholars to believe that these methods came from the Middle East. There is the work pointing out that the whole decade is missing in the historical accounts of Jesus' travels and this is explained by his long travels throughout the desert, speculating his mission all the way to India. In the most recent verified sources the Christian Templars brought this secret knowledge during their last crusade from the Ismailities sect of the Assassins with whom they fought at first and at certain point in their venture they made peace and exchange knowledge. The third story goes that St. Gregory Palamas learned body/spirit techniques in his one-year captivity, while he was held captive by the Ottomans. Spending whole year in the Ottoman prison, could he learned some of the techniques from his Muslim inmates, which is all probable and plausible, since these heretical Muslim dervishes were always a threat to the Ottoman Empire, even the Islamic Law and authorities since their first appearance in Baghdad around year 800 A.D.. Either way, the revival of this lost body/mind Hesychast meditation flourished throughout the fourteenth century in the last years of the aging Byzantine Empire. The question does remain, if the late Middle Ages revival or reintroduction of famous Hesychst body-spirit meditation is actually return to its original form, which was introduced from the early Christianity to the Middle East only to be returned and reinvented again. One of the clues' comes to us from famous and well documented Christian work "The way of the pilgrim", where there is long ongoing polemic between the Polish Steward and the Russian Pilgrim about the authenticity or historical originality of Hesychastic Meditation, where Polish Steward allude to the possible non-christian origins. The Polish Steward said that he saw this Greek Monk's meditation worked before, comparing it

with the India's yogis, making fun of it, alluding to its origins in the
Orient. The vividly disturbed Russian Pilgrim has replied the great
Hesychast Meditation is not written by the rustic Greek Monks but
by the Christian fathers of the "old-time" and has been passed down
to this time by the early Greek Monks. After all, Islam is some six
hundred years younger than Christianity so it can not be contributor
to this story of, "the fathers of the old time" and with the Messiah's
missed years from the Bible, could he really travel, as far as, India?
Recitation of the Jesus Prayer with controlled breaths, according to
some writers, even listen to the heart beats and adjusting the words
of the prayer to the beats of the heart, has very strong parallels with
most of the Hindu breathing techniques and the Islamic "listening
beats of the heart" dervish techniques among the Sufi. This breath
technique was known, even in the Christian West and the evidence
of this can be found in the famous St. Ignatius Loyola's work, "The
third way of prayer", in which Loyola proposed that for each word
of prayer one breath is to follow. Loyola proposed using technique

with the Lord's Prayer, instead of Jesus Prayer, as this was done in the known traditional Hesychast Greek Meditation. Visualizing the words of prayer, combining them with the breathing technique and placing them in four chakra body positions with the specific body pasture has unexpected similarity with yogi technique and method. It is important to note that the Byzantine's Hesychast rudimentary technique was like the baby steps compared to more complex, and elaborate methods of the Hindu yogi traditions or Sufi meditations. That does not mean that this lost original Christian technique could not find its way to the east, was broken down and improved to the more sophisticated and elaborate way in the centuries that followed. There are some similarities found in the body pastures and prayers with the Jewish mystical community known as the Merkabah, that are strikingly similar in the body postures to the Greek Hesychasts, where the body is crouched in almost fetal position and in familiar body upright, and crossed-legged positions of the Yogi and Sufi.

Method

There are several known versions of the old Hesychast meditation

techniques and since most of the source come from the polemics of

the anti-hesychast writers in the West the most common, acceptable

and favorable views of the Hesychast meditation ways comes from

Saint Gregory Palamas. The first difference from the standard and

common Christian prayer was the advice to sit on a small stool one

span high, which is about nine inches high, without back support.

This was very different from the standard Christian prayer, which is

standing or kneeling. The stool was never used by the Yogis or Sufi

of the east. Another difference was, the complete crouch in almost

fetal position of meditator's body with forehead resting at his knees

and his chin resting at the chest, which was very different from the

standard eastern traditions. At this point, Hesychast eyes are gazing

at heart that is the center of his attention throughout the Hesychast

meditation. Explore the whole heart figuratively, when making the invocation combined with the focus on the breathing was the simple method the Hesychast has employed for centuries. Despite the fact it is simple technique, there is nothing to add to it and its simplicity is the key to success. This circular position of the body, crouched in the fetal position, allows exploration of the meditator's entire body. In this position the focus is all on the heart. The second focus is on the simple breathing technique, where Hesychast takes deep inhale breath invoking Jesus name and then exhales stating; "Have mercy on me, the sinner!" Its end, the sinner was added in the fourteenth century. The other descriptions of Jesus prayer of the Hesychast is mentioned, " The control of breathing" and slowing it down. From the medical point this method is not recommended, because it does cause hypoventilation and in eastern traditions, hyperventilation or hypoventilation is practiced, again not advised, because it can have health damage to the human body. St. Gregory Palamas even stated that the body position and the breathing techniques are there to help the beginner to exercise before he got into the deeper state of high alternative state of consciousness. The Words of the prayer are to be said mentally with following the intake and the exhale of the breath. Mental focus is switched to mentally place prayer in the heart. This mental forcing the prayer into the heart with focus on the words of the prayer from the top of head, through larynx, and down to heart that exactly corresponds to the kundalini's first four chakra with its crown chakra placed on the top of the head, associated with color violet and down to the forehead chakra associated with color blue, furthrt to larynx with the green color and finally, to the center heart chakra with its red color. There was no ascending movement back to the tip of the head, like with the yogis and/or descending to the lower parts of the body that was strictly forbidden in the Hesychast prayer. Loyola in "The third way of prayer", has never mentioned the Hesychast, but he was alluding to the breathing technique, with the keeping the Lord's name in mind at all times." Remember God more than you breathe!". The original words of the Jesus prayer is: "Lord, Jesus Christ, have mercy on me, the sinner!

Color Meditation

Color Meditation has been often linked to the Kundalini System of the controlled Chakra meditation in which the particular colors are associated with the glandular endocrine system in the human body. Out of the forty two known meditations which are commonly used, we should mention only the few, which will work in this practice of psychic tuning and has benefit in its synergy with the geomagnetic Sedona vortexes. The colors are known to have healing benefits to the human psyche and body since time immemorial and are recently utilized in the West as the new healing method, known as the color healing. Sedona red rock formations in conjunction with dark green Juniper and Sycamore trees are known for their healing effect. The bright, red-orange color amplifies energies in the human mind and does stimulate the sympathetic nervous system of the subconscious mind. The dark green tree surfaces stimulate the parasympathetic nervous system just to calm the psyche and to lower blood pressure.

The colors mentioned are also influential in the human perception, and colors are consciously or subconsciously used in color healing in the West in recent decades, colors had proven positive effects on asthma, depression, circulation, coronary issues, anxiety, and even arthritis. In the Far East the colors are recognized in their relation to the energy centers that are known as Chakras, and the colors of these centers are; red, orange, yellow, green, blue, violet. Sedona natural beauty throughout the year set aside, her colors are at play and especially in the September-October time frame when most of Sedona vortexes are very active. Around Fall equinoxes, the colors influence our mind, and can be utilized in the color of the clothing we wear and food we eat are the most important visualization with closed eyes. This is important in balancing the endocrine system which is known in the East as the Chakra balancing. These are color visualization of the different energy appearances that goes through the human body in conjunction with the breathing techniques and the focus on the breath like in Zen Meditation, or the focus on the word of the prayer, like in a mantra of Transcendental Meditation, has a very powerful effect on the body and mind, especially on the geomagnetic vortex sites in Sedona at certain times of the year and at the right time the plume of energy eruptions. Red Color is center at the Base Chakra that is located at the base of spine right in the center between the lowest spinal disc and the front of pubic bone. The red Base Chakra is responsible for the grounding of the human body which means that it is responsible for the basic body/mind or the body-soul sensation of security, and the basic well-being. This warm feeling of security is what gives us the sense of relationship with the outside world and people in our daily lives. When we feel threatened by the people in our daily lives or we have problems in communication because of this insecurity sensation, then we need to work with our Base Chakra. Above Base Red Chakra, is Orange color Sacral Chakra that is responsible for the sex life, dictates our emotions and human artistic, creative lives. Orange Sacral Chakra under activity means that we have problems in our sex lives or with the lack of trust in other people. The very clear under-activity of the orange Sacral Chakra is the feeling or emotion that we are used as a sex toys by everyone and that no one loves us as we are, and wants to use us only as objects. Sacral orange Chakra is positioned a palm below the navel and the monks of the Greek Hesychast Movement were accused of being the "Navel Worshipers", that gaze at navels, while in truth they did focus their eyes at their hearts. Above Sacral Orange Chakra is Solar Plexus Chakra and corresponds to yellow is position above the navel and below breastbone. This yellow, Solar Plexus Chakra is the seat of our ego, relating to, I AM, therefore, I exist. The mid-Solar Plexus Chakra is the very center of everything which makes us conscious individuals and guards self-preservation in this World and is that primal doorway from the Base and Sacral Chakra of inner emotion-driven feelings, toward Heart Chakra that is a seat of our soul. When the Solar Plexus Chakra is too weak or not balanced we feel ruled by the others in every aspect of daily lives and our own ego is on run. The feeling that other people are always telling you what to do, with their inside ignorance of what you feel and have to say, then the Solar Plexus Chakra is in need of rebalancing. Other known diagnostic signs of Solar Plexus Chakra not working, are a constant concern of what the other people think and feel about us. The fear of Gossip is a clear indicator of lack of self confidence's negative state of mind and again the Solar Plexus Chakra needs to retune. Further up is the Heart Chakra situated that is centered of feelings, as its name indicates, and is represented with color Green, sometimes Pink. The Heart Chakra is your center, and represents the whole of you, your mind and body or body and soul. The green Heart Chakra is the emotional and self-preserve chakra, which connects us with the lower material World, and above with the higher, spiritual chakras, which lead the soul out of this World. When the heart beating stops the soul detaches itself from material world and material bondage to it and projects its own self to those higher realms, carrying what does not belong here, the thought and communication of the conscious knowledge up to higher dimension. When the Heart Chakra is out of balance, the communications with the others are blocked. Above the Heart Chakra is turquoise color Throat Chakra, which is related to dark color Blue or Turquoise and is located in the lower part of throat. This is the spokesman Chakra that is responsible for communications; verbal, written, telepathic, interdimensional. When the Throat Chakra is in its disbalance, the misunderstanding goes both ways on this and the other World. The feeling of not being fully understood or not being able to understand just anyone around is the clear indication of one's Throat Chakra is in disbalance. The balance of the Throat Chakra is very important in the mediumship work, for the reason that being unable to assert the communication with a loved one on this Earth would mean no clear communication or the blocked communication with those that have passed away. Telepathy, or receiving and even more understanding the messages could be jeopardized as well. The Throat Chakra must be balanced while we are still in this World. The Third Eye Chakra location is in the forehead and corresponds to lavender color as the seat of psychic abilities. The pineal gland is often portrayed as the Third Eye in various eastern cultures and is always almond-shaped gland, which is in connection with hypothalamus that regulates the entire body's endocrine system. Often with the clogged pineal gland which could be caused by the processed food or the fluoride water taken over the decades natural psychic abilities that we all possess may be reduced and diminished to the point of being afraid of your psychic success, have disbelief in one's own intuition. The highest of the Chakras in the human body system is the Crown Chakra that is located on top of the head and is always associated with its violet color. The violet color of the Crown Chakra is the seat of all human enlightenment and/or that spirit world and could be the portal that a person achieves Nirvana in Buddhism or to a lesser extent, Dhezba commonly known among the Sufi. There are three more Chakras that are situated outside of the human body, however, they can not be reached with this meditation.

Balancing the Chakras

The Chakra simply translates as "wheel", and it is that vortex wheel within one body. Crown Chakra is the most important one, followed by the Third Eye Chakra, in an inward or outward work, for reason that these chakras control our spirituality and lower chakras connect the human body with the outside world. Balancing all these Chakras individually and the endocrine system gives us a sense of awareness and perception, connection and rightful place on this Earth, and the Universe as a whole, thus balancing chakras as is a very important step before any psychic work. The chakra balancing should be an exercise or pre-work before the start of meditation, prayer or any other inner work. First, find a quiet place where you can do your work that can be undisturbed by sounds or lights and if you are in Sedona, find the vortex less traveled or visit your favorite one early in the morning or very late after sunset, so you can be alone. Now, sit down on the pillow in the lotus position, straight up so that your pelvis is high enough, and you could feel more comfortable. If you don't find this comfortable, take a folding chair with a back support, and sit on it with the spine in an upright position. Close your eyes, relax and imagine your Base Chakra emitting red color, between the lower tip of your spine, and your own pelvic bone. Place your hands down with all your fingers touching each other and with your palms inward, so you can make the circuit. Meditate on your Base Chakra by visualizing the red color increasing its intensity from blurred red to shiny glowing red, then make your firm affirmation that you are more grounded to this World and to all of your surroundings. Make any prayer you find useful, and at the same time reassure yourself by now visualizing an increase of the intensity of red color that you will be more the part of your surroundings with your own rightful place in this life. Continue with increasing the flow of the red color in your mind, repeating the affirmations, until you can not raise the intensity of the red color and glow anymore. Place your hands with the fingers pointing out at each other, so the circuit is made in your

Sacral Chakra below your navel and with your closed eyes imagine orange color. Examine the shade and intensity of the orange color at first, and make the determination if orange color is; muddy, blurry, with low intensity or bright and shiny orange. Raise the intensity of the bright color orange as much as you can with strong affirmations that you are open and give more love to people that you are afraid, and put more trust in them. Raise your orange color to the absolute maximum and if it is still any blurry, do not worry, you will repeat this exercise. Repetition is the mother of learning, therefore, move your hands upward between the navel and breastbone and visualize yellow color. Examine, once again, the intensity of yellow, and now ask yourself again, would you be able to make a speech without any reservations, without a worry about what your listeners would think about you, and what all the consequences would be. Do compare all your worries or the lack of them, to the color yellow in your mind. Increase color to the maximum and make affirmations that you will care less about political correctness, whatever it takes. When the yellow color is still not increasing in the strength and the brightness, make all your affirmations again, that you are in full control of your destiny. The Sacral Chakra is the center seat of your character, your ego, and your personality on this Earth. From this point, move your hands over your heart, explore the colorations, and the brightness of your Heart Chakra. The Heart Chakra's major color is green, and it could be Pink in the back. The Heart Chakra is situated in front of a spine behind the breastbone. The Heart Chakra is the place where the upper spiritual three chakras meet the lower material three. The Heart Chakra is all about love and giving, and it must be the bright green, stating that our body is in the balance with our spirit, where the exchange of love is taking place between the body's conscious self with its soul, as its subconscious self, which through the Crown Chakra reach into the higher realms of Universe. Hesychast Monks explored the Heart Chakra as their only, final ascending destination, looking for the evidence of their total surrender to the Creator. The Hesychast Jesus' Prayer moves now, from the tip of the head, then through the forehead and larynx, and down to the heart, exploring it for the answers. Increase the brightness and the shining of the green color within your mind, as much as possible as you are thinking of your loved ones. Turn all your affirmations, and the pledges of love, toward the people which have hurt you, and observe the brightness of color green. Focus on the color green in your mind, and increase its brightness and glow, as much as you could. After this exercise, take three deep breaths, move your hands up to your forehead, and change the color green to lavender. Praise your success, then focus entirely on the Third Eye Chakra, and explore the lavender color of your cat's eye's wide almond-shaped gland. Try to send the message to your loved one and possibly to the person that you share the bed with. Now, ask your loved one afterward, were he or she thinking about you around that target time, and you could be very surprised by what you found. Try to increase the lavender color of the Third Eye brightness to its full extent, above your expectation. Give your affirmation that you will increase your psychic ability with the help of the Sedona vortex energy and that you will search for your own perfect vortex site, which will increase your abilities for the perfect extrasensory communication which is that energy which you could harvest from now on. After this, move your hands above your head and visualize color violet. Make a triangle with your thumbs touch each other on the bottom and with your fingers upward. Open your triangle, separating your fingers on triangle's top, still holding your thumbs together on the bottom of the triangle and let visualization of the violet color opens up toward the sky. The Crown Chakra is the center of spirituality and the connection to the higher realms, therefore, it is the person's door to the terrestrial and celestial. The Crown Chakra has outward and inward flow of the knowledge and wisdom toward the Universe and the sea of consciousness, where you came from and to which you will return. There is no better gift than the Crown Chakra flowing above your head and glowing in it full brightness. It is referred to as the Crown Aura and if it could be detectable by the others, you have a special gift and consequently, your special duty on this Earth. Whether your Aura is detectable by the others or not do not worry, you can still access and benefit from it to your full potential. The violet Crown Chakra is, as spiritual as, the spontaneous-visionary, and if found to be dominant you will go through many periods of spiritual clarity and enlightenment. The Crown Chakra will have its full potential in those moments when the great prophets were in contact with divine and at a time, when we all could receive the messages, which will change humanity for good. The clear quartz crystal is always associated with the Crown Chakra, and beneath those red iron rusty rocks of Sedona, there are thousand tons of quartz crystal deposits that connect Verde Valley with higher realms of the Universe.

Balancing Chakras with Crystals

Gemstones have a rich tradition in Judeo-Christian tradition, which is usually overlooked. The future New Jerusalem which is depicted in the Book of Revelation has 144 square miles of exact dimensions built on the foundations with twelve layers of the precious crystals with the first being Jasper, and is followed by sapphire, chalcedony, emerald, sardonyx, sardius, chrysolite, beryl, topaz, chrysoprase, jacinth, and amethyst. These Gemstones are also mentioned in the Book of Job to emphasize all the orderly forms set by God, and in Exodus 28 where, the Lord gives specific orders for the breastplate of the High Priest to be made of a four rows of gemstones, first of sardonyx, topaz, carbuncle; and second row was made of emerald, sapphire, and diamond; third row ligure, agate, and amethyst; fourth row of beryl, onyx, and jasper, all were enclosed in gold. European traditions of using the gemstones in the visual arts and the religious statues with prayer beads were influenced by some older traditions of the Near East where crystals were used in shamanism, astrology, and healing. Specific stone is always used in cleansing, balancing and strengthening Chakras and this could be done at home or at the favorite vortex sites. The energy of the Vortex in conjunction with the crystal will dramatically amplify the results of aligning Chakra and improving the meditation. The individual crystal is associated with specific Chakra and placed above, below, or side of particular Chakra that you are working with or with the specific layout of the several stones made on them. Before any further work with crystals begins, the grounding and sensing the Chakras has to be performed. Selecting the particular grounding stone which works for you is the hardest task in this process. Many people can already feel their own personal stone that they are attracted to; based either on their own personal zodiac sign that is in correlation with the sun sign or they have already talked to the professional that selected some for them, as most people will find out, they already have an affiliation toward their personal stone based on their intuition. The grounding is one necessary step, because of any opening of the Chakra System, or the individual Chakra without Chakra being grounded or balanced, it can have the invitation of possible foreign entity, to occupy the meditator's body and/or mind which might have a dire implication. Therefore, in any great emotional distress, like divorce, loss of a loved one, job loss or any other stressful situation when we seek to reach someone or we could be vulnerable, it's not advised to open the Chakras especially not the individual ones. It is the paradox that these are the situations where we do seek out the outer work that is associated with emerging out in nature or inner work that we seek the help of the higher power or the answer to any spiritual question. Only when our inner self or our intuition tells us that we came to a closure with the situation caused by a sudden, accidental death of a loved one can and should we turn to the inner work, which includes the Chakra opening. You will know when the time has come and if you are still not sure, simply do not do it. The best stones that help with the grounding with Earth, are the Earth-colored dark stones, that include deep red, black or general quartz or iron stones above your body, as is Sedona iron and quartz, below you. Smoky quartz, Black quartz or Tourmaline work with the people, as well as, dark Citrine and dark red Jasper, also known as, Red Jasper. Sardonyx and Tiger Eye are great stones to work with the grounding as well. Jewelry made of the stones which are grounding, such as necklaces and earrings with the sharp end on the stone pointing down to Earth will help a lot since they are worn for a prolonged period. This is so critical in the time of the crisis that many amulets or the protection stones are worn. When we sense that we are fully grounded because of the feeling we are fully in our body, and if we feel no emotional distress then our attention is not disturbed. Sit in the lotus position, and place grounding stones below your feet or if laying down on a vortex site, set the grounding stone below the base of a spine. Place all the stones in your hands and hold them tight with their pointing spikes down to the ground. Placing additional stones on the throat and encouraging wandering thoughts to gather all together toward the ground. Make all the visualizations of your thoughts assembling from your mind, and push them with your mind, through your body, down to the stones, and feel the energy of your thoughts went down into earth. This first exercise is very similar to the visualization of the negative thoughts and letting them go down to the water of the lateral West Fork creek vortex stone. You have to let go of negative feelings and thoughts that will leave your body below. When you feel that you have your attention and the awareness back into your mind, turn exercise to the next level of the channeling emotions, the feelings and the thoughts of energy more down to earth. Guide your deep inhaling breath, as you feel that it collects your thoughts and feelings as it travels down to lungs, and visualize the polluted air of negative wandering emotions leaves your body as you exhale. With heavy exhaling breath make the sound "Aaah" that accompanies the breath leaving the throat and making the vibrations of larynx. After the grounding method is over, you could turn attention to balancing the Chakras with the visualization of the color method, which starts with the Base Chakra. This color visualization exercise is followed by the grounding exercise is meant to identify the blockages and the obstructions of the flow of inner, positive human energy. This inner technique of self-identification of body blockages or self-screening depends on alertness, receptiveness, and attentiveness anything that comes to mind at that moment, and analyze all the details and their meanings. It is hard to perceive that the mind can analyze the body within the body at any given moment there is the one psychological trick which helps to screen navigation and to identify abnormalities. The technique is known as the head separation from the body, or the mind from the body. Lay down on your most receptive vortex and close your eyes. Take a few minutes to focus on your breathing and now take a deep breath and count from one to ten on every inhaling breath. After counting from one to ten, countdown from ten to one, and with synchronizing of each breath with each number. Imagine your head being separated from your body on your command and with your head floating above the body and up to the ceiling, high enough so you can observe your whole body. This exercise should be done in your own room or outdoors in the Sedona's Vortex, the only natural room that is private and very secluded is the Shaman's Cave with its ceiling which encloses the actual vortex. Imagine that your whole head becomes the one giant eyeball. Now enclose your mind in your newly acquired eyeball and with this eye looked down to your laying body and now observe your body as a whole. Inspect your body Chakras and sense coloration and intensity of the colors, as you did in the past exercise.

Out of body

Color Meditation is about assessing the Chakras and balancing them with mind, tuning and pushing the blockages, eventually starting the self-healing. After lifting your head above your body, gaze down on your resting body, start inspecting it by focusing on the main chakra centers with the Base Chakra as your starting point. Visualizing the red bright color in your mind, send remotely this glowing ball of the bright light and plug it into your restful body laying down. Precisely position the red ball of light on the tip of your spine, and let excess of the bright light energy spill over, entering ground. Examine that redness of the energy and if it is not bright and glowing, but a turbid and low color intensity, think about emotions coming to your mind, and meaning of them. These emotions could be the answer to bright color associated with your red Chakra, and to negative disturbances associated with your Root Chakra. Grounding your life associated with Base Chakra establishes your deep physical body-conscious self with the world around you, which is related to the sense of the security and stability in your life. At your body base, all the small blockages associated with the Root Chakra are in correlation with circulation, and problems with arthritis, digestion, mobility which needs serious attention. The lower back pain and sciatica are clear indications of the weak and poor condition of the Root Chakra. The Root Chakra energy connects you to earth on the emotional levels. The Root Chakra could be clotted if you feel disconnected with the society and you lose the feeling of love, if you are always tired and have no energy, and if you do not feel like in your body. Carefully inspect all your emotions while you are focused on coloration of the red, and your emotions and feelings in that particular moment, you will find out the cause of it. Now, imagine the bright orange ball of lights and try to push the plume down with your mind and position it between the pelvic bones in your Sacral Chakra. Fill Chakra with the ball of orange color and let the overflow orange lights spill over it entering the ground. In this self-guided exercise, try to fill out the whole sacral area with orange color, leaving no space free of color

orange. You inspect and at the same time, find the intuitive reason

in life which causes the Sacral Chakra disturbance and disbalance.

With this technique, you are self-guided and emotionally connected

with your body, and on sublime level looking for a way out of this

disbalance. Since Sacral Chakra is responsible for every sexual and

emotional disturbance, and these disbalance will be associated with

a lack of sexual activity or the painful, unfulfilled, unwanted sexual

life. The lower back pain, arthritis and impotence, bladder or kidney

problems, and the menstrual or prostate problems with a lack of the

basic physical activity are the signature signs of blockages and poor

Sacral Chakra conditions. On the emotional level, feelings of guilt,

jealousy or any feelings that need more self-control, are all signs of

Sacral Chakra block. Examine the brightness and the coloration of

orange, as you mentally inspect your Sacral Chakra area, and think

of those immediate emotions, and the thoughts associated with your

love life, as you do mentally guide color orange through the sacral area and visualize the excess of that orange color spill over it. Try to improve the orange color with your mind, as much as you could within several minutes. Now, move your attention up to your navel, and visualize that rich yellow color filing the Solar Plexus Chakra's area. Make a dark green color enclose your chest, and let the excess of color flow out of it and then look at the intensity of yellow color, and its brightness. Since the Solar Plexus Chakra is the seat of ego or your conscious mind can direct your emotions in relations with the material world. On the emotional level the Solar Plexus Chakra is very easy to recognize, since it is connected to strengths and your ambitions, and to your material goals. In daily life acquiring wealth and material goodies is the only way of expressing success, and for that reason, any blockages of the Solar Plexus Chakra are easiest to spot. Physical heartburn and other stomach related problems such as obesity or eating disorders, are clear signs of major Solar Plexus Chakra blockages. On the other hand, emotional aggressiveness or lack of self-control, an emotional outbursts followed by insomnia and anxiety are signs of the Solar Plexus Chakra problems, as well. Using the stones like citrine, amber, chrysoberyl, and placing these stones above the Solar Plexus Chakra can improve the energy flow. The stones should be placed on the navel during the meditation, and with concentration is on the Navel Chakra, examine your mind, and see if there are any emotions or thoughts come at the moment. After you are finished focusing on your navel, move your mind up to your heart, and try to visualize the bright green color. Fill your chest area with the rich color of green energy and see what is the intensity and the brightness of green color. Again, fill the mind with color green, as much as you could and let the excess flow down your chest into the ground below you. The Heart Chakra is the seat of compassion toward other people. Your heart connects you with your spiritual self, which is your inner subconscious within your conscious mind. With your heart, you can connect with other's deep emotions and you can find your place in this material world, your true self, your place in this world. Not only that you can find the meaning of your life on this earth, but your rightful place and purpose on this Earth. Strong Heart Chakra will make you feel full of life and will make everyone around you feel better about you. When the Heart Chakra has issues, the first physical expression of the blockages are visible in the blood flow, skin irritation, allergies and emotional expression in difficulty making friends, due to a serious distrust to new people and there will be feelings of loneliness present, lack of compassion, and empathy toward others, even not accepting self anymore. Being tired of life, and place in society is the clear indication of the Heart Chakra problems. Examine the color with the emotions, and all the thoughts that come with it, think about what all these thoughts have to do with you and your daily life activities. With the power of your intuitive mind try to make the color green brighter, transparent and if possible, make it glow. Think of your loved ones and the people that brought good in your life. Use stones like jade, emerald, quartz, rose, with the color meditation and place them on the Heart Chakra, make your meditation at the Cathedral Rock Vortex or the Kachina

Woman Vortex. Pay the visit during cycles of the new moon or the full moon, since this is a special time when the moon influences the heart. Now, turn attention up to the Throat Chakra and examine the shades of blue color, your rushing emotions in regard to this color blue present. The Throat Chakra is the central connection between mind and loving heart and it is a human body window to the outside world. When Throat Chakra is blocked resentment could be present toward other people, so you would have a hard time making speech, and you would have problems telling the truth. On a physical level, you might suffer from shoulder or neck pain, sore throats, and even hyperthyroidism or hypothyroidism. Focus on your throat Chakra with your mind and try to increase the coloration blue to maximum. Think of what your thoughts have to do with your daily life activity. The inner mind examination of your body, laying down on the floor of the Shaman's Cave is now complete. Since, the examinations of your Third Eye Chakra are not possible outward or outside of your head. Remember that your head is separated from your body and it does become encapsulated within the big eye that is floating on the ceiling and in the corner of the Shaman's Cave. You are now inside your inner mind within the big floating eye and as you watch down your headless body laying on the floor. If you do not achieve your first "Out of body" experience in this head/body separation, do not worry. The purpose of this exercise is to comfort your mind that it could be without the enclosure of its body and is a preparation for any further psychic work. With the mind examine the enclosure of your "big eye" surrounding, examine coloration of blue inside your big eye. Try to enhance the color blue to be bright, translucent and transparent. Look down, to your laying body one more time and try to convince yourself that your mind will work independently of the body. Visualize you are receiving the bright blue color through your pupil into your new big eye body, and make the inner walls of your big eye surroundings by the blue glow if possible. Turn attention to the little opening on the ceiling of the inner wall of your new "big eye". Focus on your mental attention on your "optic nerve", as the "escape gateway" out of your big eye and push your mind through opening. Imagine that you push yourself through the tube in your childhood playground, waiting for the joy of seeing what is on the other side of the tube. Observe the oval window of the Shaman's Cave as the optical nerve opening that leads to and out of the eye and remember, your severed head is still there, on the floor of the Shaman's Cave and try to assure yourself you will come back to it. Observe Verde Valley through the Shaman's Cave natural circular window and look around Verde Valley and endless ocean of violet colors, vibrating in all different shades of violet in motion of light mingling down the Valley' floor. Inspect now color violet with its glowing brightness, and fly with your mind through the violet air, making the circle. Make sure that you come back through the oval window of the Shaman's Cave and that you come back through the enclosure of your big eye's opening. Observe briefly the blue color around you and like a paratrooper pick up the blue color and move through the pupil of the big eye toward your body. Enter with your mind into your laying body through your neck and keep both your eyes closed. With the eyes closed, take several minutes to feel your neck, your shoulders, and your breasts. Take as much time as you do need to feel the upper parts of your body and do not open your eyes. It is important to understand that you do feel yourself back in your body right before opening your eyes. Now, move down your hands, and feel all your fingers, count each one of them, and then move to your legs. Move your legs, feel them, proceed to your feet, and do the same, slowly open your eyes. Look above the ceiling of the Shaman's Cave and then slowly move your head, and examine your surroundings. Since you have returned safely from your astral travel with the several exercises like this will dramatically improve your psychic ability which you already have, but which are pushed back by constant assurance on the part of your conscious mind that dreams and daydreams are irrational part of our own minds. In the bizarre head/body separation it is very important that you can train your mind in which the conscious self should be severed from your subconscious self. This is why people have symmetrical minds, like two eyes, two lungs, two kidneys, two parts of the brain. Everything in the human body is Asymmetrical, joint but separated at the same time, and controlled. The subconscious mind could get loose, be all independent, free of conscious mind, its attachment to body senses, therefore, all your six senses will be unobstructed to explore further. These laboratory studies do suggest that remembering dreams and motivation to retain, as much information as possible, is crucial to building up the extra sensory perception abilities and this will work with daydreaming as well. The advance commitment to remember your dream is very important in reviewing the dream or daydream during meditation, as well as, talking to your partner, pre and post, dream sessions. Writing the dream diaries and the meditation diary will help build your psychic skills further. Meditation daydreaming is often associated in the most eastern cultures to the art of a ritual dying. In its core essence, meditation is the practice of letting go of the physical attachments of one's body five senses or the conscious awareness of all surroundings, letting go of the subconscious mind and make it free wandering around. The subconscious mind makes the astral travel and exploration in many different realms, with the quantum leap in many different dimensions with breaching the time and space, therefore, going to the future or the past. The person who experiences a near-death situation in the laboratory study, with the induced out-of-body experience, and willingly subjected himself to severed head from the body separation self-hypnosis will build the lifelong psychic awareness skills that will stay forever. Remember, the stubborn persistent repetition and the will to reach your psychic skills that are always there but only forgotten, will come to fruition. Meditation helps to sort through five senses of your physical body and to detach your conscious mind from the awareness of physical body, to pull and build your psychic abilities and to straight out of your subconscious mind, where it has been buried for a long time.

There are numerous schools of meditation in the Jewish traditions, however, the one that is the most popular in the non-Jewish circles is the ancient tradition of Kabbalah practice, that has been a form of Jewish mystical practice that is present from time immemorial. Compared with the Greek Hesychast tradition and the Kundalini Meditation in Hinduism, it has some amazing parallel that can be drawn. First, all the written records came from twelve century and do contain elusive secret knowledge used by most mystics in their inner circles. It refers to the seven days of creation and knowledge that was first given to Adam, explained as the "Tree of Life", that correlates to creation, from the smallest atom to the complexity of the human body and mind. Symbolically it is visualized as the tree grown with the positive connotation, yet in the Christian Heritage, it has the negative association as the "Forbidden Tree" from which Adam and Eve were not to eat. Referring to God's creation, all the levels in the Tree of Life are going down from its divine source in ten levels called sephirots, and since the tree of sephiroth is parallel the actual number is seven, which exactly corresponds to the seven Chakras. The Sephiroth is the station where God manifests himself in the one station or in all of them, and creates the human body in a very symbolic way. Sephiroth can be accessed in an ascending way, so that the Man could access the divine source where it came from, and should be united with his own Creator. The Kabbalist meditator who seeks the meaning of life, would start meditation with the first sephiroth called Malkut that always correspond with the Base Red Chakra which makes a circuit with Kether, correspond with Crown Violet Chakra and is the seat of the Kingdom of God on this Earth. The Kabbalah meditation starts from the base and it ascends to the highest Sephiroth, enlightenment in one's spiritual life and climbs the Tree of Life. The actual root of the words Cipher and Decipher come from the word Sephiroth, which is decipher of meaning of a life through the ancient Jewish Art based on numerology or the art of reading words through the numbers. The meditations along with prayer could go in an ascending, descending and crisscross ways in a complex grid of numbers, that brings the meditator to the answers he is looking for. The Sephirot next in an ascending way is Yesod, that corresponds to the Sacral Orange Chakra, often referred to as the "mirror of mirrors". There is no surprise that this is referred to as biological functions of life. The whole Solar Plexus Chakra area is covered by two Sephirots; Hod is to the right side, and Netzach to the left side. Hod holds all learning, trade, travel, and speech, while Netzach holds instinct impulses that could be harvested after a long meditative period that does lead to more discipline, and ultimately toward wisdom. Tiphereth translates as Beauty and corresponds to the center of the Tree of life or the Heart Chakra, and it is the seat of lower and upper Sephiroth. The Throat Chakra area is almost all covered with the dual, upper two Sephirots; Geburah/Justice which is to the right and Chesed/Mercy which is to the left in the tree of life. Geburah/Justice always adds Chesed/Mercy with a judgment, and Chesed returns to it with obedience and the rule of law. Daat is the Sephiroth above that does not hold space and is the precursor to Ajna, known as the Third Eye Chakra. Datt for that reason does not have its number and it symbolizes the unification of the knowledge between right and left human brain (Corpus Callosum). The Brow Ajna Chakra or the Third Eye Chakra has link with the Sephiroth is represented with the Binah which is (understanding) to the right of the Third Eye or the Ajna Chakra, and Chokmah (Wisdom), to the left side of pineal gland. The Binah to the right is the seat of your left brain thinking or the male brain, where the rationality and the reason take place and is the central location of our inner conscious Self, mathematical, analyzing and rational Self which observes and changes this World. Chokmah to the left of the Brow Chakra is the seat of a right-brain, subconscious thinking. The Feminine or right brain is responsible for the visual arts and music, the dreams and visions, its subconscious connection with Divine and divination. The Kether or Crown Sephiroth is a place where everything starts and ends in relation to creation symbolized as the lightning bolt and rest of the Tree of Life as the God's Creation on Earth. The Crown Chakra is that portal that unites The Tree of Life in the human body with its source, the rest of Universe, and with other trees across the Globe. Kabbalah schools have different approaches to interpretation and practice of the Arts of Kabbalah. The approach does come from the fact that Kabbalah itself has different traditions coming from the three different texts that are fundamental in Kabbalah's history, and from the one simple fact that Kabbalah's secret oral traditions are passed to the initiate by the word of mouth since time immemorial. The texts of Kabbalah are composed in time immemorial and are called; Zohar, Sephir Bahir and Sephir Yetzirah. All scholars agree that the most prevalent source for classic Kabbalah is Zohar, which was made in the thirteenth century and most possibly on the basis of the older tradition, Sephir Yetzirah that is much older, and dates back to the origins of this Jewish tradition. The Oral tradition was passed down mouth to ear for simple reason of concealing Kabalah secret teachings, but also for the reason of letting the initiates and

students of Kabbalah find the answer on their own, since Kabbala

deals with interpersonal unification with their Creator, the World,

and whole Universe. The Kabbalistic Tree of Life was the first grid

where the spiritual life answers can be found. This personal, inner

exploration of the Tree of Life starts with a grid of ten Sephiroth's

in the shape of the emanating spheres, with the hidden Daat, which

is the 11th Sephiroth that criss-cross 22 paths, connects Sephiroth's

representing the Hebrew letters on three pillars, the foundation of

the Tree. Combinations of Sephiroth's and the paths between them,

33 in total, resulting in the repetitive emanations of God, therefore,

exploring the true nature of his creation of the Universe, World and

ourselves. The number 32 represents 32 levels in the human spine,

with 33 being the hidden location of Daat. The horizontal lines on

the Tree of Life divide the creation of the Tree in its Four Worlds,

and which is very similar to the Four Worlds of the Hopi Creation

Mythology. The Tree of life is the map God created in all possible ways, the grid that could and should be more explored in personal meditation, and found the answers we all seek from Creator. In the Gnostic Christian texts when Peter asks the Lord; "My Lord, how shall we recognize Thee?", the Lord has answered; "Peter, lift any stone and you shall find me there!", and " Whomsoever will find the true meaning of all these words shall not perish, but shall live forever!" Meditate on the Tree of Life, explore its branches, with your eyes closed, visualize the "Tree" or use one of those Twisted Sedona Vortex Juniper Trees as the personal grid for your answers. On Sedona Vortex sites, you will find one or more Twisted Juniper Trees which are twisted and swirled by Vortex of the geomagnetic fields, coming out of the Sedona stones. Above the Wind Tunnels, there are four Juniper Trees, each can represent The tree of life.

Intuition

Intuition is often seen as rudimentary, atavistic, reptilian ESP which we acquired from the animals in the evolutionary process of human history and passed down to the future through what the evolutionary psychologist Julian Jaynes called the Bicameral Mind. In time when people were able to build a great civilizations, but at the same time were much more dependent on that inner voice that is called, the gut feeling or hunch, that passive form of ESP, which we call intuition. The inner voice of intuition is still there, however, intuition is a part of the subconscious mind which has been put asleep by conscious mind where we are awake. Our bodies are made of bi-symmetrical alignment in a way that we have only two kidneys, two eyes, two lungs, two hemispheres of the brain, therefore, two separate minds, subconscious vs. conscious. When we are asleep, our subconscious mind is let loose and conscious mind is asleep. When we are wake, our subconscious mind will go to sleep and conscious mind takes over. Despite that, our organs are working simultaneously, and it is not so with our minds. The children up to twelve years of age, have more imaginary minds and they often create imaginary friends and see things that adults do not see. Psychologists explain this as the normal process in childhood development and clergy explanation is that the children have more open connection with the divine before they become the corrupt adults, but if there is any more to this? This transition to adulthood in traditional societies throughout the world is much longer than in the developed industrial societies, this is due to the educational system and media. Anything spiritual, including the psychic work is deemed as childish, immature, from the point of any organized religion, the psychic is labeled as the sorcerer and for this reason, everybody pushes psychic aside. The dream was always recognized as a muffler for the soul, therefore, as not of the rational cognitive thinking, which is based on the reason and interpretations of all the precognitive dreams as the pseudoscience. From this point on, we have always been school trained that we should push all our deep feelings, emotions and dreams, as not real and with insisting on them to be a part of reality, we do risk rejection from the society, which we are part of. The people often choose to push subconscious information deep down and instead working with it, we consciously bury it. As we get closer to the golden retirement age, when we are niether threaten nor ridicule at the school or workplace, we become confused with this new freedom, which we find for ourselves in our interpretation of dreams that come true or with instant hunch, a gut feeling, which becomes reality in our near and sometimes, instant future. We discover our new old imaginary friend as an inner voice that we labeled gut feelings, hutches under the new official name, intuition. The most intriguing fact is that intuition comes and goes and the most stressful feeling is that, no matter how much we try to control it with our cognitive mind. This can be very stressful for the most successful people in a society, so they just clock out for good. When they find themselves in new reality, the most successful men die within three to five years after retirement and there is a reverse correlation between the society's most successful individuals and their longevity. The exceptions are males with that deep feeling of "Letting Go", which provide them with a long life gift, because it does help them to bridge between their conscious ego grip and the subconscious mind as a messenger of soul revealing itself. It has been known that the more successful person insists on rejecting the inner voice of his or her soul to reveal itself, the more that person's conscious mind suppresses the subconscious mind. The best action is just to accept intuition as the genuine spokesman of the soul, as that old, imaginary friend that came back and leads you to a joyful and long fruitful life. Intuition is in fact that six sense that we have acquired when we were born and we carry that gift throughout life. Intuition has been suppressed by the society and anything that has been deemed as an imaginary is regarded as the childhood atavism, is almost always suppressed by our reason-driven or school trained mind. Prof. Julian Jaynes believes that Corpus Callosum has been more porous in recent human evolutionary past. This joint point or

Corpus Callosum has been much more open to information transfer between two brain lobes not only in human's evolutionary past but in young children under the age of twelve. Information sometimes shoots through the Corpus Callosum in adults as well and in some of those moments when human mind is too relaxed, the inventions came to fruition. Some of these all-time famous inventions are, for example, Archimedes famous bathtub "Eureka " incident and Albert Einstein's ideas, during some of his shaving sessions is attributed to this. At this moment when the one's conscious mind is relaxed, like in a bathtub or with morning shaving session, one's conscious mind allows most information from the deep subconscious mind to pass all the way through barrier of the tissue between Corpus Callosum, resulting in the greatest World inventions to come around. Intuition has been let loose from the subconscious, and passing obstructions of consciousness, being accepted in that fateful moment, as the true message from soul, it does become reality. It is known that women are more intuitive than Man, and this can be supported by the facts that the estrogens, play a role in the right brain lobe, and estrogens somehow in their unknown way slow the left brain thinking, letting intuition run free. Creativity, visual arts, music and writing, are the fields closer to women and are all under the influence of right and often called, female brain. It is important to stress that the women's inner ears are rich in magnetite that play a role in being receptive to the geomagnetic fields and information from far beyond. Intuition is a far more superior to all the other forms of ESP because it has been linked with creativity and action. Intuition is a precursor to all ESP; premonition, precognition, clairvoyance and mediumship, however, unlike in the passive information, which may or may not be used by receiver, intuition calls for an immediate action and is a life-saving event. Intuition does not have to be discovered, intuition is already there and it can be sharpened by meditation or dowsing. Ask simple yes or no question inner self and you will get a quick answer in any possible personal situation that may arise with the help of dowsing pendulum, will build the intuitive abilities of the mind. Raise those questions that you have at the geomagnetic vortex fields, which will amplify your intuitive answers ten folds. Using material items, such as, dowsing pendulum, quartz crystal balls, rune stones at the vortex site with an urgent inner need to find the answers will yield positive results. Visit Sedona vortex during dry summer months dry winters, solstices or spring and fall equinoxes and early in the mornings and very late at night. Use secretion of pineal pigment melatonin at its peak between two and five A.M. and during time of the full moon, when the geomagnetic fields are the most active will help develop and sharpening the intuitive skill. The food to be taken prior to the vortex visit should be rich in amino acid tryptophan, the precursor to serotonin-melatonin chain reactions in this chemistry of human brain that will help melatonin release in a natural way. Tryptophan rich foods are; turkey meat, spinach and pumpkin seeds.

Pendulum

The pendulum is a great helping tool for intuition awakening from the subconscious depth buried by decades of conscious suppression. Pendulums are made from metal, stone, glass in all kinds of shapes, and sizes, but if you acquire one made of the quartz crystal or iron, it does conductive transmitting, just like the rust and quartz of that Sedona dirt beneath your feet. The pendulum tool gives the answers from, your subconscious intuitive mind without the interruption of your conscious mind. Pendulum is the tool which extracts most of the information your conscious rational mind asks in a way which tricks your conscious, like if you ask someone else or any outside source, like God or angels, believing that your subconscious takes no part in this conversation. This gives intuitive subconscious the only chance, perhaps in decades, to reveal itself free of its constant conscious suppression. The pendulum can give you only yes or no answers to the rational mind question but is the most efficient tool in rediscovering intuition and building one's first and new psychic skills and eventually even accessing the Hall of Records from some other dimensions. Akashic Hall of Records is the Universal Library which is accessible to all Humanity and to every individual that can access it with its subconscious mind, and being able to do so, will find the proof of humanity's union with the Universe and all other human beings. This is the ultimate goal of being one with humanity and the Creator Himself. Using a personal pendulum tool is the first "baby step" which you will never overcome, but will stay with you for the rest of your life, even in the most distressful and disgraceful situations it will be there for you so you can get you quick answers. Remember that most life-saving situations require quick and almost instant answers in the field, and because of the panic mode that your conscious mind is caught in. There will be no time then, when you can use meditation techniques, and your intuition might be blocked, caught of guard at the moment, but you would have your pendulum near you. The pendulum is more like the Kachina dancer Mask, one quick tool for accessing your hidden subconscious inner self, that

the Kachina dancers call the "friends". Pendulum as weight on the

string must be pointed down on the target, which may be an object

of the missing person, another person's body in healing technique,

for cleansing of the Chakras. However, if no material object is to

be used, a plain piece of paper with a circle drawn in the form of

target is sufficient enough. The string that Pendulum is hanging on

should be some twelve-inch long from the pendulum cone to your

hand, one inch away from the target paper. From here, concentrate

your mind on making Pendulum stay still with a sharp point above

the target paper. Make the command with the words in your mind;

" Stay still!" Repeat this three times:"Stay still! ", because this is

crucial part in using your Pendulum, when you tune your personal

vibration with an object of the Pendulum. You use your conscious

mind to ask the questions, but since your focus is on the Pendulum,

your conscious mind is self-tricked into alignment with the object,

and the "Higher Voice" will give you an answer, from the depth of your subconscious mind. When you find you are completely sure that the Pendulum is still with its point on the target, your next step is to find out what your Pendulum movement answer can be, "Yes" and "No". Ask yourself well-known polygraph questions, such as your name, your birthday and surely Pendulum will make a move. The Pendulum work is a fun exercise, but it is the precision and the accuracy depends on preliminary alignment. The pendulum would make a move slightly clockwise or counter clock direction and only this should be your positive answer. If you think that the pendulum gave you yes answer that is exactly what the technique is supposed to make you achieve with a conscious mind, tricking yourself into the belief that the pendulum or other outside source gave you an answer. The answer to your questions does only come from your intuitive mind, your subconscious, and this is just, great start. As you get better with your pendulum techniques, your six sense will get better too and your conscious mind will get used to allowing your intuition to wander, and you've just broken the ice. Now ask your pendulum the question that you know the answer will be no. At this point, you have just broken down your pendulum device and you know which direction the pendulum will move with the answer yes, what will be its move for the answer no? When you work with your first pendulum next time, you still have to do the calibration or tuning of your pendulum, clockwise or counterclockwise movement of your pendulum can be very different. In the deep meditation the work we do is self-hypnosis or putting our conscious mind to reset, prompting subconscious mind to work without interruption. In any pendulum work the idea is to trick our own conscious mind into the belief that someone or something else gives us the answer-question, not your soul, therefore, it allows a subconscious to do its intuitive work. Pendulum is only the clairvoyant training tool, it would not predict the future in detail, rather it will only give you simple, true answers without even involving, interfering consciously. The man consciousness never lies and that is why the saying, " Trust your gut! " does exist. The pendulum could only answer the question;

"Loves me or loves me not? ", without interfering in often "foggy" conscious that play smart with real you, your heart. The pendulum is your personal polygraph in the emergency situations when you do need quick answer your own pendulum will be telling you the truth, and the truth shall set you free. Keep using your pendulum as a tool to get your daily life important answers, and you can keep them in the dream diary. Make two pages, where you will list the questions about your daily decisions and your rational conscious mind answer them on the first page and write those same questions on the second page and use your pendulum to answer them for you. The next day, review and compare the initial answers to those questions and what is all your pendulum answers. Compare the answers to the decision you have made the previous day and you should be very surprised. With time, you will become an expert in using your new polygraph by testing your friends or your co-workers, eventually your spouse. Ask the first person in your surroundings the "picky" question you estimate will yield you the incorrect answer. Especially target those personalities known to be pathological liars and for the test purpose intentionally accept answers as being truthful. Now use a pendulum again, and ask your pendulum if "John" was lying to you answering the target question. From now on, you should be more intoxicated with your newly rediscovered polygraph and you will be carrying it with you in your pocket for the rest of your life. Remember that in the most stressful situation when an immediate answer is demanded you will not be able to mediate and your reason conscious mind will block your active psychic centers for this brief moment but you will have your new pendulum for the quick answer. Use pendulum at the Sedona vortex and see if your answers will come more quickly with more emotional charged answers.

Premonition

Premonition is sort of an ancient internet of the universal telepathy between close people who form the emotional bonds based on true love, and compassion. Premonitions are often found between those immediate family members or lovers, but may be extended to even larger social groups, which give them warnings in the time of crisis. Premonitions are those warnings which may help you save your life and are an instant feeling that you should take a different road while you drive or just not to take the trip as you did intend. Premonitions between you and your loved one are those, often a very painful gut feelings that the loved one is in danger, half a globe away and often felt by their mothers, and very well documented in the time of war, whereas the mother would feel inner instant pain when her son was hurt, injured or died. Premonitions often come in the dreams about the event that is about to happen, which can affect the entire nation, say a forewarning dreams for several weeks before the 9-11 attack.

Premonition could be revealed about any large or important event incoming within a week or less, due to that important event which is of concern to you or your loved one, and usually happens within the hours or the minutes in awake state or the day before, often in a dream. This explains why the large scale events which could affect the larger social groups amplify the vibrations of the messages that come to the people in their dreams or in awake state. Since, people are telepathically connected, the vibration messages take off like the tsunami wave, which is getting larger and larger. Amplification of a vibration message eventually is so large that its surge can be felt by many ahead of its time, like the earthquake among one social group. Premonitions always do come true and it is very hard to avoid them, and unless there are directed and of your personal concern, you will instantly react to your gut feeling, and suppress the one's conscious mind ego, thus the premonition could save your life. The control of the one's premonition is a skill that is very hard to master, but like with anything else in life you will master it by repetitive techniques, such as affirmation and letting go of ego, your conscious self. This is not mastering skills through control, on the contrary, this is the master skill of letting go of it all. In all meditation techniques of a self-hypnosis you could, actually, ask your conscious mind to step aside, go to sleep, and as you progress with your inner meditation, the ability of your mind to withdraw itself will be easy, sometimes in an instant. This is all to it and as you do master the technique of letting go, you could be more predisposed to let the premonitions come in your life in that critical moment that might be life-saving. Therefore, premonition can't be controlled since, one's conscious mind is set aside and can not be called up, but will be there for you in the time of need. Sometimes, premonition is in the form of the symbol, which could play a role in your spiritual tradition, try to call yourself, again from another plane to guide you through your dreams, and play an active role the next day in protecting you and your loved ones. This call will result in a premonition that turns to precognition.

Precognition

Precognition is the actual abilities of a person to predict the future, and see the past, which is called post-cognition. On the contrary to the popular belief that the precognition skills are reserved only for the people who carry the natural gift that they are born with, or they inherited it from their parents or grandparents, the psychic ability is there for everybody to harvest it. Just like in any art, this is all up to the person's will, wish, work, and persistence of the effort how well this ability will be mastered. The dream journal is a great tool and it is used, along with the gift of accessing that information through the precognitive dream. This technique is based on putting the rational, conscious mind to sleep, and accessing the source of subconscious mind in awake state, with divination techniques which are used to access the same source through the material objects, with frequent conductivity of Mother Earth, such as in Sedona vortex, is a way to achieve the same goal. Unlike premonition, that is a passive event giving warning sign of concern to you or information of concern to your loved one, the real precognition is active channeling of one's subconscious mind that can give you a reading of your future event, and affects the person to whom we do a reading for, and sometimes the larger social group. The precognitive event may be days or even decades away and often comes in one's dream, or in the divination material, tarot cards, crystal ball, tea leaves, runes and subconscious mind wandering through space and time extracting the information. The reading which is close related to precognition is post-cognition which always involves the use of psychic time travel to access often missing person or a dead body, often using an object that belongs to the missing one, and therefore accessing their energy vibrations left over in that one object. Often police use this post-cognitive service from the professional psychics when most other resources had been exhausted. Sometimes even the psychic which has been hired to do the reading can become the suspect, depending on the information extracted, which is available only to the murderer and there have been many instances where one sheriff would hire the best psychic to do a psychic job and the other sheriff will become suspicious of psychic knowing too much. The best way to start with training your precognitive skills is already described by keeping a dream journal. The passive way of using dreams as your precognitive guide is the way of extracting the information when you are not prepared for the precognitive dream flight. Anticipating the particular dream comes through the following night and with focus on the information that we want to know about ourselves and the near-future, it is crucial to ask the anticipated question your higher self about the outcome and the consequences of our role in particular dangerous situations that may arise in regard to our finances or love relationships like closing a deal, test at school or even possible life-saving event. Before the anticipation of what is to come is to ask your subconscious mind to reveal the future, and anticipation must be followed by affirmation. Your affirmation that the will future reveal itself is nothing else, but asking your conscious mind to believe that your subconscious will do the job without conscious being involved, therefore, asking your conscious self to stay aside and let your deep subconscious do this work. Human relationships are built on the belief that the conscious should not trust subconscious, since relationships should be guided by rational reason like everything else in organized society. When the conscious trust is lost, the marriage could be lost, therefore, the one's conscious mind can not afford loose navigation of one's own life and let subconscious sail on its own. The affirmation allows and gives confirmation by the conscious that the subconscious has the permission to wander into a dream and give us the information that we desire. The ritual before the dream function as an official order by the conscious to the subconscious to go ahead and reveal all the information on its own and is, as important as, any long affirmation in the form of prayer and could be, as simple as, preparing a cup of chamomile tea. The informal rituals before sleep, such as brushing teeth or simply combing hair, can be used as the formal ritual, like drinking chamomile tea, which sanctify the intentional affirmation.

Trivial and naive as it may look like, this little ritual along with the intentions, affirmations and anticipations is important for successful precognitive dreams and so are awakening and recording the dream itself. There is a crucial time, when remembering the dream, before opening your eyes, immediately write it down in the dream journal. Translating this acquired behavior, in the day-dreaming meditation technique is, as important as, using last night's precognitive dream. First, start the meditation with relaxation of your body in a straight, upright position, cross-legged, preferably on the meditation pillow, so that your pelvis is slightly elevated. Close your eyes and take ten deep breaths, imagine that on each exhale breath, your body moves a foot back on the moving pillow. After that, just imagine that your magic pillow moves you ten days in the past on each exhale breath. Do not hold your natural breathing, and try to record the image or photo of your past ten days and exhale breath briefly. Shuffle now, through these images and try to remember them so you could write them down in your just newly acquired day-dreaming journal. You are training your post-cognition of your past ten days, which is far easier than your precognition, because of your inner conscious self believes, knows and approves your reading, since the events have already happened, most important it has been approved by inside, conscious self. What you do, is just letting your subconscious mind scoop up any possible images that slip through your conscious self-review of your past ten days. This meditation daydreaming is very similar to a self-hypnosis which is exactly what meditation is, and people under hypnosis remember the facts and the events that they could not remember with their slow conscious slippery minds. You would be very surprised of, just what your first-time, post-cognitive daydreaming meditation will reveal about the people and the events you actually missed and all their most important picky details. After the counting back from ten to one in correlation with your exhaling breaths, review and more importantly, write down images that you could remember. Use the same technique for your precognition day dream by counting from one to ten in association with incoming ten days. Relax, sit upright cross-legged, and close your eyes taking the deep inhaling breaths. On each exhaling breath do imagine that your meditation pillow moves a foot forward and a day ahead and if you see any images which come to your mind, no matter how ridiculous may be, often images come in the form of symbols. Open the mind to incoming images, and try to remember them in association with the numbers which you are counting. The incoming images will be accepted by your conscious mind, since you have already done the post-cognitive reading that is accepted by your ego, because what happened in the past ten days. You have just reviewed your past ten days, and sorted through the past that you are convinced happened, and you are just sorting out, right? It is far easier to sort through the next ten days, that you are anticipating? This is absolutely crucial, since you have tricked your conscious mind with the post-cognitive reading in precognitive reading that might just come true and it will come true! You have to open your mind to this slight possibility without convincing yourself that you have to believe it or to know it, however, this openness is crucial to become a psychic. This is the first and the most important stepping stone for you to overcome and after that, possibilities are endless. With this method, you will soon find out that your pendulum, your tarot cards, and your crystal ball will not be as necessary, because you would be able to access your future at will, with no tools. Your tool is there to help you in your journey and your favorite Sedona vortex will be there, to help you out with her geomagnetic, iron rich quartz crystal field. The Vortex will be there to help you with the question but the answers will not come from the vortex or your pendulum, these answers will come through you and only you because you are vortex. Tune this inner vibration of energy in your body with the geo-magnetic field of the Earth vortex in the nice dancing alignment with Mother Earth, and the result will come emotionally quick but this is you which is your first channel of the information revealed before you, about you and your loved one. For the people who can accept that they are the one and the most important person which will happen in their lives and want to share this most important find in their lives with the others

the benefit will just amplify. The first psychic reading and guided

meditation in the groups are easier and much more beneficial to the

individual and to the group alike, and the results would reveal quick

and easy, since the expected anticipations, intentions, affirmations,

and expectations can amplify the synergy of this vibrational energy

summoned in the one. The Sedona vortex vibrations pieces together

this information on the large scale and turns the precognition into

the premonition, concerning these large events, can not be changed,

even the premonitions concerning close individuals of that reader

never change, there were meant to be. The understanding in which

the premonitions are superb to precognitions should be engraved in

stone, since they give those psychics advantage in changing future,

and while it is still in the form of precognition. We can see all new

events as they unfold in the sequential way, one after another, rarely

we can point to the exact day and time, and this school of thought

tells us that the time is an illusion. We could prepare for any future events by doing precognitive reading every day with the hope, they do not turn into the premonitions, where the surge of this energy is so strong that the wheel of life cannot be turned back. Even small scale premonitions which might come as a life-saving hutch can be too little too late, a split second information of an event that could turn wrong if we let our ego make decisions. Therefore, one should always rely on its gut feeling, since it will not let you down. Most importantly, you could do your meditation and your reading daily, and do not turn away from the pendulum, your tarot, your crystal tool whatever they may be. Visit Sedona, if you could regularly, especially in the time of need, Mother Earth should never let you down for you are part of it, do not turn your back to vortex, it is there for you.

Telepathy

Telepathy is defined as the mental communication between two or more entities and is easily tested with close people in personal life and works the best with the person who is willing to work with you on this. The easiest telepathy approach should be with your positive intentions, expectations, affirmations, and persistence, and this will yield positive results. One partner acts as the sender and one as the receiver. The sender should be one of the partners who is proactive, controlling, more creative in the mental projection of visual images, whether they may be the colors or symbols. Projecting those colors and symbols are the easiest way of sending the telepathic messages since these patterns of the sensible messages are condensed into the colors and symbolic images that summarize many messages into the pattern of one. Later messages could be more complex, and broken down in more detail, in the form of the rolling movie story. Try now telepathic communication with your partner, agree on the time and shorten your exercise to less than ten minutes. The longer exercise lasts, the less accurate results will be, because your consciousness does interfere with subconsciousness and the accuracy of the result goes down with time. Your partner agrees that your target time will be High Noon and will last for ten minutes. With mutual agreement, your conscious mind will expect, agree and allow subconsciousness to the target exercise. Split the exercise in a way that partner sits on, the Airport Mesa Vortex and you on the Boynton Canyon vortex at High Noon and agree, who will be sender and who will be receiver, and agreement should be made who is sending the color messages, in the order one to ten. You will be amazed by the accuracy of this telepathic exercise. Try this again, with the symbols, use a deck of cards with random spades, hearts, diamonds, clubs mixed. Sender should align them in order of their symbols and colors. Sender will concentrate on sending the mental images precisely at a time agreed and the receiver should be focusing on these images and write them down.

Scrying

Scrying is an old method that has been used for millennia and it has been known for reading the desired messages from the past or in the future, such as, looking into a crystal ball, a ball of water, or reading tea leaves on the bottom of the tea cup. Scrying subconscious mind information from the past or the future with your cognitively aware conscious mind occurs in the moments when the two minds are not communicating with each other by no other means but medium that recall reflection in the crystal. This is the moment of reflecting the holographic images captured by conscious mind and scrying for the information which may happen in any gloss medium, such as shiny metals, oils, water or glass windows under a certain angle. It seems that the viewer's own conscious mind, under a certain angle is able to pass through the multiple dimensions of time/space capturing all the reflections of this irrational multidimensional subconsciousness which is still present in numerous dimensions at times. The crystal ball or other medium is a place where this breakthrough is present spontaneously in a quick moment, we refer to the reading. Reading takes patience in a matter of an hour or within a day and many days of constant tuning, but when the image occurs, the next reading will be made in a shorter and shorter time. The paradox of scrying craft is that it can not be achieved by inforcing or pushing the conscious mind to make it happen, on the contrary, the inability of conscious mind to see it right away, will end up in frustration, and give up in disappointment. Putting conscious aside and letting subconscious wander, just like in the meditation, will lead to success. Before any scrying, the personal affirmation and the expectation must be made with full belief in the success, and patience and persistence must be present throughout the sessions. You should choose one quiet and dim place, and place the crystal ball in the center of the table on its stand. Lights should be turned off and a small candle lit in a corner of the room to provide the small dim light. Focus your mind on the depths of the ball, passing the surface, like you are diving into the water, and expect to see the fog or mist forming in the interior, like cigarette smoke, and when this cloud occurs you will be in the right way. The fog appearance may take a day or two of your gazing until vision occurs, and this is where your patience will come to fruition. Dive through the fog in the deeper interior you will see nothing but empty darkness. This picture might not be clear until several days pass of the intense and stubborn gazing, but when they do, the next scrying sessions will be short and with the better quality of images. Reading the round crystal ball or bowl filled with water can provide only general information about the events of concern to individuals and in relation to the whole community and it is very different from tarot or tea-leaf reading when the reading is of concern to particular individuals in its immediate surroundings. The crystal ball gives the information that is rather premonition at first and as the major event unfolds before the reader, the premonition will crystallize into the precognition during the crystal ball reading.

Mediumship

The soul that has not passed on the other side, either because it did not want to pass and were resisting the fact that the body gave in or the individual suffered violent death and has a need to tell its story will reveal itself, especially to the loved ones. This communication is called mediumship and people do exist who are born with the gift of being medium and can communicate with everyone beyond their grave at will. Mediums are people that are gifted psychics, because every psychic is not a medium, but every medium is a psychic. The mediumship along with precognitions are the hardest skills to learn and to master unless the person is a natural-born medium, however, it is possible to learn, acquire and to master the medium techniques especially in the well-trained groups. Those spiritualist movements and groups which we know from popular movies and books were flourishing in the past, with their secret group gatherings until this craft has become abused and manipulated with charlatans seeking material gains that forced the whole movement to fade away. There are still spiritual churches active throughout the United States, but the movement is a far cry what once is used to be. Today, readings are performed by the professional mediums in their, "one on one" reading, in which a medium is channeling communication between the loved ones who are seeking interaction. There are professional mediums in the Uptown that would perform the channeling for you but being on that special vortex that you are the most responsive to, this channeling will happen to you in the direct communication with your loved one, who seeks your direct attention or with the one to whom you have to say something you have missed in this life. Just like with premonition channeling could be passive, with or without the invocation and it does depend actively on your strong need to make contact and bring this broken communication to closure. You have to find the vortex that you are the most responsive to, then just sit in upright position, relax with a deep inhaling and slow exhaling of your breath, while you do focus mentally on the visual image of the person that you need to talk to. With your persistence and strong will, you should mentally call up your target person with visualizing the person image and the call will yield a positive result. Sometimes the image will show only as the distant silhouette ot sometimes you will be involved in the direct communications and this depends on the soul passed, as well as, your urge to get this communication on going. The major obstacle to this most of the time is when the one's soul is confused with its own status since it has been stripped from its earthly cloak body and the communication ends up with the one question sentence, such as: " What are you doing here? " or with: " Where are you? " It depends on how far the soul has advanced through its journey and how strong is soul's wish to communicate with you words it had no chance to speak in order to make closure. The clerics and psychics that I talk to, always discourage all these communications with the passed ones, for the sole reason that the freed soul needs to find its undisturbed path to the afterlife, and for the sole reason that you can disturb or confuse them in the journey.

Your loved ones would sometimes make an active communication with you often in your dream or on the vortex site when you are in the most relaxed state of consciousness. The soul have urgent need to make this final communication and affirmations that the soul is doing well and soul wants to speak the words which he or she has missed to say, in this life. The position that you will take could be, strictly personal, and there is no advice to this, but it is important to stress out that the process of the passing is not completed within first forty days or more after its passing and if you have something to say or your loved one has to add something the communication should be done within this short period after that person's passing for the benefit of passing itself, and for the benefit of the soul that needs to rest and not to be disturbed in their final journey. For this reason, the prayer for the dead is very common and is present in all religious traditions in order to help the soul in its final journey. The paradox of communication using the medium is that the soul does need an undisturbed journey, however, the soul also needs the final closure of the communications with a living loved ones, therefore, whatever I have to say to the people that passed, I do it within this forty day period after their passing. After that, I do not call them anymore, unless they come in my dream, seeking communication with me and even then, I do not ask many questions, I only try to listen, and somehow make the meaning of the words and need for this communication. The passed one will never ask for the current events, since the soul is disconnected from the most of the events which are no more of concern for them. These communication are usually limited for their need to tell you they are well. Sometimes the passed ones will just try to reveal themselves if they have to warn you about the event that may be of concern to you in your own passage and this appearance is usually affirmative and often calming in nature. In my most recent experience, I had very clear communications at the Baby Bell vortex location and the Kachina Woman Vortex in Boynton Canyon. Most of the active medium's communication is just linked extension of those communications between the two people in this life, and far beyond it. This should be treated and held in privacy, strictly and only personal, therefore, there should not be advice for the future. For the passed ones, this communication serve the purpose of reassuring the living that they are well and they will meet them again, and for the living this last communication serves as the chance to say a final goodbye, and say the words that has not been said, and for both this is an expression of assured everlasting love. Sudden unexpected passing of a loved one is the most frequent cause of any ESP experience, and visiting geomagnetic active grounds, such as the Sedona Vortex do amplify this experience. How you would like to utilize this experience is a strict personal choice, but it is important to know that your visit to the Sedona vortex after passing of loved one and will dramatically increase your mediumship and communication, that we all possess. The iron rust, which is infused with the basalt layers and limestone that the Sedona rocks are made of, in conjunction with the quartz crystal layers deep down below your feet, and number of massive caverns with impressive underground rivers flowing from the San Francisco Peaks, make Sedona unique red ground interdimensional portal. Channeling through this portal in the Sedona rocks will just amplify all your ESP gifts that you already have, from intuition to telepathy, channeling to mediumship, it is just how willing you are to use this amplification natural pools of energy for the benefits of you and your family. Being at the right time of a day, such as after dark or before sunrise when melatonin release is strongest, taking the foods rich in tryptophan, such as spinach or pumpkin seeds will increase the experience. The time of a year, such as the equinox or solstice, and the evenings of the full moon should also increase this experience. Your favorite tools, such as a pendulum, tarot cards or the small crystal balls can help as well. Soon you will find out that you will not need them.

The Sedona Field

What are those true connections of the geomagnetic fields, and the ESP experiences phenomena reported by the thousands of people visiting Sedona, and the hundreds of psychic residents that gather here to make Sedona the permanent address? It seems the Sedona story started million years ago when a volcano under Sedona left a few dozens of large empty shafts and hundreds of smaller shafts branching from mother shaft, like the big Juniper underground tree. What used to be filled with lava are now empty tunnels that allow the plume of geomagnetic energy flowing up in a spiral, creating a wind tunnel in that old shaft we refer to as the vortex. Influenced by the Sun and the Moon, the movements that push the vortex of geomagnetic plume up flow and especially at time of a full moon during equinox and solstice. It has been proven that on all these special days of the year large geomagnetic field is predisposed to disturbances, and because of the openings in the Earth's crust, the plume of geomagnetic energy shows in the hundred thousands of locations throughout the Planet Earth and Sedona is just one of the locations, location with a hundreds of shaft openings. The U.S.G.S maps are available for the public on their website with Arizona and Sedona in particular and are marked as high geomagnetic activities. In the Earth's outer core is molten lava that is circulating the Earth inside crust that is only responsible for a majority of inner Earth's magnetism and is keeping the Earth "alive", and well protects the Earth from the Solar Flares or Solar Storms, which would "burn" the Earth without protection of geomagnetic field. Geomagnetism is responsible for gravity and it is keeping us on the safe distance orbiting our Sun. The lesser influence of Earth's geomagnetism is attributed to these special features of the inner core of the Earth, such as Sedona volcanic shafts, and even to possible atmospheric influences like the Solar Flares and distance from the Sun and the Moon during orbit. The lunar cycles of the Moon have their effect on the tide of the seas and thermal currents in Earth's atmosphere, and is well documented that on full Moon nights, some individuals are more sensitive in positive or negative manner, and their psychic abilities are enhanced in their dreams or in their awaken meditation sessions. More of these geomagnetic disturbances are reported in all the cycles of the Sun explosion flares that happen at times, but it is active during the years which always repeat themselves in ten-year cycles. In ten year cycles, the Sun gas explosions are emitting more radiation towards the Earth, and in collisions with the geomagnetic field of the Earth, produces an extra geomagnetic activity in forms of the plumes. The collisions are happening all over the World, and particularly are active in opening cracks in the Earth core, and are responsible for the hypersensitivity of humanity as a whole and the result is that in some years the World has more conflicts and wars than the rest of that decade. Some spots on the Earth are known as Vile Vortices, and these locations are well-known as; the Bermuda Triangle, Dragon Triangle in Pacific Far East, the Vile Vortex in the Algerian Desert or in parts of India, etc. The maps of these Vile

Vertices are readily posted online, as well as, the hundreds of good

vertices listed on the web the Vortex Hunter. Decades of research of

all the geomagnetic disturbances in the laboratory, as well as, in the

field resulted in the find that all days after the highest geomagnetic

activities, are followed with the dive of this activity to lower levels,

and it is exactly on these days of the very low geomagnetic activity

are followed by the high outbursts where the small amplification of

PSI abilities are enhanced with general population of a people who

are seeking their psi experience or trying enhance their spiritualism.

The Geo-magnetic activity is a term used to describe the oscillation

of the geo-magnetic fields influenced by the solar flares eruptions

and collision of solar emissions with the natural geomagnetism of

the Earth. All these measurements take the highest measurable field

with the lowest measurable fields around the globe and producing

the index, that should be applied on all the local geomagnetic field

measurements, as well as, the global index expression. The portable equipment is applied in all measurements of the Sedona's Vortexes done by electro-engineer Ben Lonetree with the tri-field monitors, flux meter, and the other Gauss meters to obtain the data, which is published on his website called, "The Sedona Effect". The research has been done in the laboratory and in the field came with positive results in passive psi; clairvoyance, precognition, premonition with the ordinary people experiencing them spontaneously and with the meditator's more active ones, like a psychokinesis. The measurable numbers in Sedona are an example of a local geomagnetic activity that causes the PSI passive experience. The measurements, which were taken globally shared between the world's observatories were taken to obtain the global geomagnetic index, and it is known that these disturbances in the global geomagnetic fields are happening every decade with one period that can last the whole year or longer. Dr. Michael Persinger has found out that this lower geomagnetic field activity enhanced spikes in spontaneous telepathic abilities in most of his patients on the years with lower geomagnetic activity.

Dr. Persinger found that a low geomagnetic activity has resulted in the enhanced remote viewing, with a precognition and premonition dreams. Sometimes this interval of measurable active geomagnetic field can last whole decades like in the period between 1870-1879, and the longer like in 1890-1909. Dr. Michael Persinger was curing his epileptic patients in the eighties with small magnets, and over time Dr. Persinger created a device which is popularly known as the "God's Helmet". The "God's helmet" can be purchased online, and this is an ordinary helmet which is infused with magnets where all the electrical impulses are sent between these magnets, causing the artificial electric charged magnetic movement stimulation temporal lobes of the brain causing spontaneous psi effect. In most laboratory experiments, passive receptive psi will always occur during the low geomagnetic activity followed by the days of the high geomagnetic activity. This is the case with his patients and with a control study, regular people, however, it is important to stress that those people with long meditation experience with minimum of twenty years in meditation will have psi experience during the high spikes of those geomagnetic active fields. It has also been found that women are more responsive to geomagnetic activity and it is believed that this must be due to some eighty-five percent metal magnetite found in the human inner ear, which is atavism we inherited from the animal kingdom. This magnetite is responsible for the birds' migrations and their astonishingly accurate navigation that is linked with magnetite alignment with the Earth's magnetism and the Earth's poles. This is found among some mammals, such as dolphins, which gives them the same compass accuracy abilities. Women are known for having the better psi ability even when they are not trained as professional psychics, and this is simply known as the `Women's Intuition". The scientists in the field agree that magnetite plays a role in navigation of the intuition skills with the individuals who have more magnetite. All individuals possess some magnetite to a certain level, and this makes us all potential psychics some with more talent that could be much more receptive. In laboratory studies with the God's Helmet, almost all individuals can experience the psi effect, while epileptic patients would be even more predisposed to it; experience do range from astral travel to out-of-body experience. Sedona's geomagnetic vortexes will enhance and amplify this experience with exception, that we could not control the switch bottom, which Mother Earth does. How much magnetite in the human tissue is responsible for the God Helmet effect is still widely debated, but the conclusion is; geo-magnetism of the Earth or laboratory induced geo-magnetism, has an effect on the human body and so far, the magnetite in inner ear in conjunction with the temporal lobes of the human brain, will induce PSI activity. The first findings of a magnetite in the human tissue was conducted at Caltech Pasadena research facility, back in 1992. These Pioneer studies have been done by Joseph and Atsuko Kirschvink and for the first time found the traces of magnetite in the human tissue. Before this it was known that the tissue magnetite is present mostly in protozoa, bacteria, birds, as well as, dolphins and whales. Using superconductive magnetometers, most researchers have found between 5-100 million iron magnetic crystal in a variety

of the human brain tissues. Examined by TEM, or transmissions of

electron powered microscopy, and electron diffraction, the scientists

find most of them resembling those in the animal tissues. Summary

conclusion of these studies is that; the small ferromagnetic crystals

interact more than a million times more with the external magnetic

fields than the diamagnetic or paramagnetic material of the similar

volume, and the earth's magnetic field could yield many responses

that stand above the thermal noise (Kirschvink J.L. 1992 Phys. Rev.

A 460). In these laboratory studies, most average magnetization of

the brain tissue resulted in approximately 4 ng of the magnetite per

gram of brain tissue. These findings were not conducted in order to

find a side effects in the form of elevated PSI, rather the focus was

to identify the magnetite in the human brain tissue that does yield a

positive results showing that the magnetite crystals were identical

with those found in the animal brain tissue and are responsible for

the animal navigation and detecting earthquakes. This study focus on the MRI clinical applications, and the effect on the human brain tissue and weaker magnetic fields are produced by the large electric power lines and the small household appliances. These microscopic particles or the clumps under the electron magnification aggregated toward the magnetic finger device that was the only one producing and simulating the magnetic field. Receptiveness in the laboratory studies can be transplanted in Sedona's vortex geomagnetic fields, despite the lack of the closed laboratory-controlled environment. It is possible to track the geomagnetic oscillations of a vortex energy and their first effects on the meditators and psychics in the studies performed by Ben Lonetree electro-engineer and Sedona's resident. Other research which is conducted by scientists; Ghosch P., Jacobs, Kirschvink, and Cisowski, resulted in the link found between rock magnetism and the human brain magnetite activity. The tissue cells were infused with the crystals of biogenic magnetite and is named, magnetocytes. Scientists found out these brain's magnetic crystals were interactive with most rock samples. Just one magnetite crystal will cause the neighbor crystal in the active magnetic field to make distinctive shifts (Cisowski, S. 1981). These effects were present in all animals and in human tissues including the brain tissue, showing the multiple interactions. The magnetite crystals present in the rock sample formations in a minimum of 50 to as much as 10,000/each cluster. In the human brain tissues, on the other hand, there is only one cell per 5000 of magnetite crystal clumps (McNeil, Kirschvink 1993). Research studies confirm magnetocytes are normally present in the animal and human tissues and are not created by the outside environment. In the study conducted by Ghosch in 1993, traces of magnetite were found even at the end of T-lymphocytes that play a major role in the human immune system. Many Sedona's residents claim they feel better sitting on the geomagnetic vortexes and even improving their health. Research in this field is not conducted yet, but the number of people who claim the self-healing on the major Sedona vortexes is staggering. The biological role of magnetocyte in the human brain tissue is unknown but in the migratory animals magentocytes help with navigation by detecting the geo-magnetic

field and the animal crystals is linearly aligned in the chain which

lacks in humans. It seems that, at some point in time of the human

evolution some people used to possess this navigation abilities, as

well as, the sense for incoming earthquakes, which is lost to time,

and if it was found in certain individuals this would be atavism. So

far, we do have the indication that magnetite infused with the brain

cells may play role in the PSI phenomenon and with the temporal

lobes of our brain pick up the inter-dimensional information of the

geo-magnetic field with its highest concentration in the American

Southwest, and particularly in the Sedona area. The Sedona vortex

passive psi experiences are influenced by the Solar flares, notably

by lunar cycles but it is also dependent on seasonal plumes activity

of the Sedona vortexes which are very active on the Solar equinox

and particularly on the Fall equinoxes, and to a lesser extent on the

Solstice with less activity from the end of May to the beginning of

July. The one seasonal effect on the strength of a PSI activity was first noticed by scientists Sturrock and Spottiswoode in 2007, in the lab study and just one decade earlier Spottswood found there could be a very specific relationship between the passive PSI activity and sidereal time. Sidereal time is always measured relative to position of the stars and on fall equinox, when the sidereal and local time do coincide, sidereal time begins to recess 4 minutes a day, therefore, PSI has the strongest activity on September 20-21st and has to have some correlation with the local time and sidereal time coinciding. It seems that this "time-lapse" in average psi reading is the strongest on September 21 st since, coinciding of both times come close, and make this PSI effect of the interdimensional information possible in timeless space. Teleportation of the PSI information is known to be related to the Moon cycles, and it was in 1973 when scientist Ante Puharich found the intense PSI telepathy activity during Full Moon days. The precognitive dreams are dramatically frequent during the Full Moon nights, and the lottery winnings were enhanced as well.

Third Eye

Third Eye Ajna Chakra or pineal gland, aside of magnetite present in the inner ear and throughout the human brain tissue plays major role in PSI phenomena in general, and especially in geomagnetism enhanced situations. While magnetocytes or the cells in the human brain provide the fine alignments to vibrations of the geo-magnetic field of the Earth, and to increased magnetic activity of the Sedona Vortex, the temporal lobe may play a different role. Persinger in his theory confirmed in laboratory setting that both temporal lobes of the brain produces a micro-seizures in the parts of the brain called the hippocampus and amygdala, which resulted in a big increase in PSI abilities. Located between the two temporal lobes, it is Pineal gland which produces pigment melatonin that regulates the sleep cycles and provides the final end product, DMT which is the most potent drug known to man. DMT hallucinogenic drug was found concentrated in San Pedro Cacti, and has been used by Indians of the Southwest in the shamanic rituals for centuries. Being known to the U.S. Federal, and local State Government as a substance, which is an illicit drug, San Pedro Cactus has been banned for a long time and recently has been allowed in the Shamanic Ceremonies, on the basis of religious freedom. DMT is the same end product found in the South American plant called Ayahuasca. Pineal gland produces DMT in traces, if it is nourished with tryptophan rich foods, if you visit the geomagnetic field vortexes, especially in certain times of the year and day. Visit the vortex between 8 pm and 4 am when the secretion of its pigment melatonin is higher and meditate with your focus on the breathing technique, intention, affirmations and prayer. Eating foods rich in tryptophan, such as the pumpkin seeds, spinach and turkey will prompt tryptophan releasing into the chain reaction. The chemistry of chain reaction goes; conversion of tryptophan to 5-hydroxytryptophan by same tryptophan hydroxylase enzyme and 5-hydroxy tryptophan is converted into serotonin by the aromatic amino-acid-decarboxylase enzyme. Both serotonin and dopamine are those "happy hormones" released in the pineal gland, serotonin is acetylated-methylated to make enzyme melatonin. Melatonin's highest production is at 2-4 a.m. and it is no surprise that the art of scrying and the tarot reading had been associated with the nocturnal lady's craft. In deep sleep, CO_2 is withdrawn from melatonin with sleep hyperventilation that can be induced prior to meditation. The deeper we take the breath during meditation or in deep sleep, most melatonin will be produced, hence, with vivid precognitive dreams will be revealed. In conclusion, visit the Sedona Vortex September 20-21st equinox nights, when melatonin natural production is high, and meditate with breathing technique that is synchronized with the prayer and above all, give affirmations, expectations, visualize the target person or event, have faith in yourself, and you will have the PSI experience.

Vortex for you

Sedona had drawn people for decades with a different expectations of what they would find. Some two-thirds of people, stated that they visited Sedona with an expectation to find a spiritual enlightenment, peace of mind, pray or simply get the professional psychic's reading in Uptown Sedona. One-third of Sedona visitors said, their primary reason for Sedona vacation is; golfing, rock climbing and mountain biking; some said they came for their romantic getaway but none of them would in advance reject vortex story. Some negative reactions have been skepticism mixed with curiosity, however, everyone that visited the Airport Mesa Vortex site, if nothing else, said that this is the most beautiful scenery on the Earth. Many have visited the Red Rock State Park to take a photos of the most recognizable views in the American Southwest. The Pink Jeep Tour is hard to miss during your Sedona visit and helicopter rides to Verde Valley, sometimes with an extended flight to Grand Canyon. The Verde Valley train's tour start in Clarkdale and the Pink Jeep Tours with the helicopter rides is the fantastic way to learn about Sedona. The limo tours of Verde Valley wineries is available for the wine lovers that come for the tasting, that is voted to be the most romantic small town in the whole United States. Sedona have a lot of restaurants, cafes, pubs found throughout uptown and many offer live music events. Many of the art galleries populate Sedona, especially in a part of Sedona that is called the "Gallery Row", is close by Sedona bridge and the main intersection called the "Y". One-third of the Sedona visitors say they visited Sedona for reason other than spiritual, but none of them would ever come back home without, at least learning about the term, Sedona vortex. Many sarcastically call Sedona religious Disneyland, mocking the town's reputation, but no one deny that Sedona is very special and the most beautiful place that they have ever seen. Some two-thirds of those who knew why they are here in Sedona, and what they will find when they meet with her deep secret, sole question, why they are here, becomes irrelevant. Love will be there, for those waiting to find the lost relationship which will flare up in their hearts and calm the souls with the promise of everlasting love that is beyond the body senses, which connects the dead, the living, and those yet to be born. Sedona is the portal, the channel and key to the inner dimensions that offset the space and time as we do perceive with our five senses, therefore, gives us the very unique opportunity to tune to time travel. Sedona connects us with loved ones that pass our body senses in four dimensions, and able us to see the future and past, harvest that information which may benefit us along the way. Learning to channel and to connect with the other dimensions through the dreams, as we have seen, is not so hard or complicated task, given the tools, and the meditation techniques. Knowing what Sedona offers and utilizing the acquired abilities will help you to find the inner peace, give the closure, and some sense of deep understanding of what you already are in your dream state, a true psychic.

Bibliography

Cordell, Linda S. Archeology of the Southwest 1997 Academic Press San Diego Ca.

Colton, Harold S. 1946. "The Sinagua: A Summary of the Archeology of the Region of
Flagstaff, Arizona, "Bulletin 22. Museum of Northern Arizona, Flagstaff.

Colton, Harold S. 1956 "Pottery Types of the Southwest, " Ceramic Series 3c. Museum of N. Az

Pilles, Peter Jr. 1979. Sunset Crater and the Sinagua: A New Interpretation. Academic Press NY

Pilles, Peter Jr. 1996. The Pueblo II Period along the Mogollon Rim. University of Arizona Press.

Bostwick, Todd W. Byron Cummings: Dean of Southwest Archeology University of Arizona Press. Tucson Arizona

Christy G. Turner, Jacqueline A. Turner Man Corn: Cannibalism and Violence in Prehistoric American Southwest University of Utah Press. Salt Lake City UT.

Harold, Courlander: The Fourth World of the Hopis. Crown Publishers, Inc. 419 Park Avenue South New York, N.Y. 10016

Noble, David Grant: Ancient Ruins of the Southwest. Northland Publishing Company, P.O. Box 1389, Flagstaff, AZ 86002

Hoffman, Enid: Develop Your Psychic Skills. Schiffer Publishing, Ltd. 4880 Lower Valley Rd. Atglen PA 19310

Papus, The Qabalah: Secret Tradition of the West, Samuel Weiser, Maine 2000.

Bailey, Alice. Esoteric Healing: A Treatise on the Seven Rays. London: Lucis Publishing, 1972

Blavatsky, H.P. Isis Unveiled: Secrets of the Ancient Wisdom Tradition, Madame Blavatsky's First Work.Abr.Ed.Wheaton, IL: Quest Books, 1997

Cayce, Edgar. Reincarnation and Karma. Virginia Beach, VA: A.R.E. Press, 2005

Hall, Manly P. The Secret Teachings of All Ages, New York: Tarcher, 2003.

The Way of the Pilgrim, The Jesus Prayer Journey-Annotated and Explained, Translation by Gleb Pokrovsky, 1954, 2001 by SkyLight Path Publishing, Sunset Farm Offices, Route 4, P.O. Box 237 Woodstock VT 05091

Lonetree, Ben. Sedona Synch, Geomagnetic Brainwave Synchronization, 2010

***